The Pla

meal plan

A 21-Day Meal Plan To Eat Well Every Day, Lose Weight Fast And Get A Healthy Life

Winona Hext

© Copyright 2019 by Winona Hext - All rights reserved.

This eBook is provided with the sole purpose of providing relevant information on a specific topic for which every reasonable effort has been made to ensure that it is both accurate and reasonable. Nevertheless, by purchasing this eBook you consent to the fact that the author, as well as the publisher, are in no way experts on the topics contained herein, regardless of any claims as such that may be made within. As such, any suggestions or recommendations that are made within are done so purely for entertainment value. It is recommended that you always consult a professional prior to undertaking any of the advice or techniques discussed within.

This is a legally binding declaration that is considered both valid and fair by both the Committee of Publishers Association and the American Bar Association and should be considered as legally binding within the United States.

The reproduction, transmission, and duplication of any of the content found herein, including any specific or extended information will be done as an illegal act regardless of the end form the information ultimately takes. This includes copied versions of the work both physical, digital and audio unless express consent of the Publisher is provided beforehand. Any additional rights reserved.

Furthermore, the information that can be found within the pages described forthwith shall be considered both accurate and truthful when it comes to the recounting of facts. As such, any use, correct or incorrect, of the provided information will render the Publisher free of responsibility as to the actions taken outside of their direct purview. Regardless, there are zero scenarios where the original author or the Publisher can be deemed liable in any fashion for any damages or hardships that may result from any of the information discussed herein.

Additionally, the information in the following pages is intended only for informational purposes and should thus be thought of as universal. As befitting its nature, it is presented without assurance regarding its prolonged validity or interim quality. Trademarks that are mentioned are done without written consent and can in no way be considered an endorsement from the trademark holder.

Table of Content

Why I Wrote This Book 1

Book Description 3

Chapter No 1: Introduction 6

    Why a Plant-Based Diet? 7

    Starting a Diet and Weight Loss 7

    Advantages/benefits of Plant-Based Diet and Its Usefulness 9

Chapter No 2: Create a Plant-Based Diet Using a Meal Plan 11

    Foods Allowed and Not Allowed 12

        Food Allowed 12

        Food Not Allowed 12

    Stress Management and Mindset 13

    Myths and Misconception about A Plant Based Diet 14

Chapter 4: 21-Day Challenge and Beyond 16

    Plant-Based v. Vegan v. Vegetarian 17

    Pros and Cons of a Plant-Based Diet 17

    Frequently Asked Questions 18

Chapter No: 5 21 Days Meal Plan Recipes (Total Recipes126) 21

   Core Practices Good Habits 22

   Day 1 23

      Breakfast 23

         Orange French toast.. 23

      Lunch.. 26

         Coconut Cauliflower Curry 26

      Dinner... 29

         Dinnertime Vegetable Soup 29

      Snack 32

         Roasted Chickpeas.. 32

      Drink /Smoothie... 34

         Tropical Smoothie 34

      Dessert.. 36

         Double Chocolate Cupcakes 36

   Day 2 39

      Breakfast 39

         Chocolate Chip Coconut Pancakes................ 39

      Lunch.. 42

         Healthy Green Soup 42

- Dinner 44
  - Tacos with Salsa 44
- Snack 47
  - Gluten-Free Pistachios 47
- Drink/Smoothie 49
  - Avocado Banana Smoothie 49
- Dessert 51
  - Lemony Oats Cookies 51
- Day 3 54
- Breakfast 54
  - Eggless Scrambles 54
- Lunch 56
  - Simple Veggies Stew 56
- Dinner 58
  - Green Gram Split Lentil Recipe 58
- Snack 61
  - Cauliflower Poppers with Sauce 61
- Drink/Smoothie 63
  - Blueberry, And Almond Butter Smoothie 63
- Dessert 65
  - Raspberry Brownies 65

Day 4 68
  Breakfast 68
    Breakfast Blueberries Pancakes 68
  Lunch 70
    Garlic Pasta 70
  Dinner 73
    Roasted Cauliflower Soup 73
  Snack 75
    Banana-Oat Protein Balls 75
  Drink/Smoothie 77
    Beets and Berry Smoothie 77
  Dessert 79
    Plant-Based Mug Cake 79
Day 5 81
  Breakfast 81
    Panini Recipe 81
  Lunch 83
    Quinoa Lime Burrito Bowl 83
  Dinner 86
    Rosemary Balsamic Roasted Vegetable 86
  Snack 88

Dark Chocolate Figs 88
Drink/Smoothie 90
  Smoothie Bowl 90
Dessert 92
  Quinoa Pudding 92
Day 6 94
Breakfast 94
  Mushroom, Olives and Chickpea Omelette . 94
Lunch 96
  Tomato Soup 96
Dinner 98
  Instant Pot Acorn Squash with Cranberries . 98
Snack 100
  Herb-Crusted Asparagus Spears 100
Drink/Smoothie 102
  Chocolate Protein and Strawberry Shake ... 102
Dessert 104
  Cherry Soft-Serve Ice Cream 104
Day 7 106
Breakfast 106
  Whole-Wheat Berry Muffins 106

Lunch 109
  Chickpea Cauliflower Quiche 109
Dinner 111
  Indian Peanut Noodles 111
Snack 114
  Peanut Butter and Chocolate Bars 114
Drink/ Smoothie 116
  Raspberry Creamy Smoothie 116
Dessert 118
  Pumpkin Oatmeal Muffins 118
Day 8 120
Breakfast 120
  Mason jar Overnight Oats 120
Lunch 122
  Cold Raw Peanut Soup 122
Dinner 124
  Zucchini with Stuffing 124
Snack 126
  Carrot Cake Oatmeal 126
Drink/Smoothie 128
  Fruity Smoothie 128

- Dessert 130
  - Easy Brownies 130
- Day 9 132
  - Breakfast 132
    - Oats Pancakes 132
  - Lunch 134
    - Avocado Toast 134
  - Dinner 136
    - Tofu and Peanut Satay 136
  - Snack 139
    - No Bake Oatmeal Bars 139
  - Drink/Smoothie 141
    - Snack Time Smoothie 141
  - Dessert 143
    - Homemade Chocolate Ice-Cream 143
- Day 10 145
  - Breakfast 145
    - Triple Berry Porridge 145
  - Lunch 147
    - Tofu Tikka Masala in Instant Pot 147
  - Dinner 150

Simple Spinach Soup 150

Snack 152

Strawberries Popsicles 152

Drink/Smoothie.. 154

Green Smoothie Recipe 154

Dessert.. 156

Dessert Time Parfait..................................... 156

Day 11 158

Breakfast 158

Keto Cinnamon Coffee 158

Lunch.. 160

Baked Veggies with Sauce 160

Dinner... 162

Coconut Cabbage Stew 162

Snack 165

Fat Bombs.. 165

Drink/Smoothie.. 167

Sunrise Smoothie 167

Dessert.. 169

Keto Vanilla Custard 169

Day 12 171

Breakfast 171
  Savoury Cauliflower Bread 171
Lunch 174
  Pasta Salad 174
Dinner 176
  Zucchini-Mushroom Bowl 176
Snack 178
  Herbed Potato Hummus 178
Drink/Smoothie 180
  3 Berries Smoothie 180
Dessert 182
  Keto Vanilla Pannacotta 182
Day 13 184
  Breakfast 184
  Raspberry Truffle Brownies 184
Lunch 186
  Broccoli Lemon Pasta 186
Dinnerr 189
  Sweet Potato Soup 189
Snack 192
  Raw Broccoli Poppers 192

Drink/Smoothie 194
   Classic Smoothed Recipe 194
Dessert 196
   Chia Seed Pudding 196
Day 14 198
   Breakfast 198
      Lemon Muffins 198
   Lunch 201
      Tofu Chow Mein 201
   Dinner 203
      Vegan Tacos 203
   Snack 206
      Strawberry-Mango Ice 206
   Drink/Smoothie 208
      Chocolate Peanut Butter Shake 208
   Dessert 210
      Cinnamon Spiced Apples 210
Day 15 212
   Breakfast 212
      Vegetable Pancakes 212
   Lunch 214

Lunchtime Rice 214
Dinner.. 216
Noodle-Free Pad Thai 216
Snack 219
Walnut Squash 219
Drink/Smoothie... 221
Mango And Pineapple Smoothie................. 221
Dessert.. 223
Pecan Ice Cream 223
Day 16 225
Breakfast... 225
Instant Pot Blueberry Coffee Cake.............. 225
Lunch... 227
Creamy Carrot Soup..................................... 227
Dinner.. 229
Green And Potatoes With Corn Dressing... 229
Snack 231
Chickpea Avocado Salad............................. 231
Drink/Smoothie... 233
Green Banana Smoothie 233
Dessert.. 235

Pumpkin Tart With Oat Crust 235
Day 17 238
Breakfast 238
Banana French toast 238
Lunch 240
Zoodles with Tofu And Peanut Sauce 240
Dinner 243
Roasted Potatoes 243
Snack 245
Eggplant Dip 245
Drink/Smoothie 247
Raspberry Almond Chia Smoothie 247
Dessert 249
Carrot and White Bean Vegan Blondie's ... 249
Day 18 252
Breakfast 252
Banana Bread 252
Lunch 254
Zucchini, Corn, Soup 254
Dinner 256
Vibrant Turmeric Coconut Rice 256

Snack 258

Cauliflower Chocolate Pudding................... 258

Drink/Smoothie.. 260

Kiwi and Kale Smoothie............................... 260

Dessert... 262

Cornmeal Waffles... 262

Day 19 265

Breakfast... 265

Baked Oatmeal Cups..................................... 265

Lunch... 267

Orange Black Bean Taquitos 267

Dinner.. 269

Rise Sweet Potato Dinner Rolls................... 269

Snack 271

Eggplant Caviar 271

Drink/Smoothie.. 273

Melon-Mango Smoothie............................... 273

Dessert... 275

Raw Chocolate Coconut Cashew Bars 275

Day 20 278

Breakfast... 278

- Vegan Breakfast Skillet 278
- Lunch.. 281
  - Quinoa Gado-Gado Bowl 281
- Dinner.. 284
  - Vegetable Spaghetti....................................... 284
- Snack 286
  - Sushi Salad 286
- Drink/Smoothie.. 289
  - Grapefruit and Pineapple Smoothie 289
- Dessert... 291
  - Sweet & Salty Healthy Dessert Bars........... 291
- Day 21 294
  - Breakfast 294
    - Banana Teff Bread.. 294
  - Lunch.. 296
    - Harvest Vegetable Instant Pot Minestrone. 296
  - Dinner.. 298
    - Low Carb Easy Soup...................................... 298
  - Snack 300
    - Chocolate Chip Cookies 300
  - Drink/Smoothie.. 302

Strawberry-Orange Smoothie 302
Dessert... 304
Peach-Cranberry Cobbler 304
Shopping List for 21 Day Meal Plan 306
Shopping list 306
Conclusion 315

Thanks again for choosing this book, make sure you leave a brief review on Amazon if you like it, I'd really like to know what you think.

Why I Wrote This Book

I wrote this book to help a lot of people like me. My story is simple; I was obese and found it hard to maintain a healthy weight. I found it difficult to stick to a restricted diet plan which omits some large food groups. I was a foodie and loved eating. I couldn't focus on healthy eating habits, because no matter which diet I chose to follow, it had a lot of food restrictions. Then my co-worker told me about a plant-based diet.

In the beginning, giving up all the junk food items like pizza, refined sugar, white rice, and some beverages seemed difficult, but with proper planning and a lot of alternatives to choose from, I now feel confident following a plant-based diet.

After adopting this diet, I was free to choose what I wanted to eat, in contrast to some other diets. I just start identifying healthy food. For snacks, I eat nuts, fruits and drink a smoothie. I love eating meat, and the plant-based diet allows me to enjoy meat as well as dairy.

The plant-based diet is the lifestyle that I have adopted and am following for the long term. Its benefits are huge; it helps me lose weight, and I feel more energetic. I wrote this book to encourage all the people out there and to help them achieve their weight loss goals.

Let's hop in for a mouth-watering journey.

Book Description

Are you looking for easy weight loss and weight management? Are you interested in eating those food items that help prevent certain recurring illnesses? Do you want to put a lighter footprint on the environment? Then the plant-based diet is just for you! This comprehensive cookbook is all that you need to get healthy, fit, and lose weight in no time. It has a lot of healthy and plant-based food options. The plant-based diet has been around for a long time, and you can't deny its well-known benefits and advantages.

This book is all about the basics of a plant-based diet: its benefits and how to practically implement the diet by following a 21-day meal plan, including recipes to help you to get started. This cookbook is perfectly suited for those who do not know what to and what not to include in a plant-based diet, and how to make changes in shopping habits. It clearly defines the type of food items you need to buy.

In modern society, people indulge in bad eating habits involving junk food; as a result, obesity has become a leading health issue. For all those beginners or people who want to lose weight and try some healthy food alternatives, but need help with where to begin, this book will serve you well.

The aim of this cookbook is to help all the people make positive changes in their life that are not only inexpensive, healthy and easy, but also enjoyable. Once you start reaping the benefits from this diet, there will be no going back.

This cookbook provides you with all the necessary information, skills, and knowhow to change to this diet. The recipes included in the 21-day meal plan are divided into segments like breakfast, lunch, dinner, snacks, smoothies /drinks, and desserts to ensure the transition goes smoothly. The exact nutritional values are given with the recipes. If you are ready to make changes in your life, then jump into the 21 days journey with us. This is the right time to do it. The plant-based diet is a very nutritional diet that will help you lose weight and stay active and fit. This book is more than a recipe book; it is a guide to a plant-based diet.

This book is categorized into sections, including 126 recipes:

- Solid reasons to follow a plant-based diet
- The food suited for the diet

- Simple and easy directions for each recipe
- Energetic breakfasts
- Main dishes
- Tasty lunches
- Fantastic smoothies and drinks
- Low calories salads and snacks
- Scrumptious desserts

Now, let's get started.

Chapter No 1: Introduction

This part deals with everything you need to know about the plant-based diet to start an effective 21-days weight loss program, including over 100 delicious and mouth-watering recipes.

The plant-based diet is a style of eating that focuses entirely on food from plants. Foods in this category include fruits, nuts, seeds grains, legumes, vegetables, oils, and beans.
The plant-based diet is different from a vegan or vegetarian plan because a plant-based diet doesn't forbid eating animal products; it allows you to choose a more proportionate amount of plant-sourced food in your diet.

People understand and use the phrase plant-based diet in a variety of ways; a lot of people take the name literally. For most of those people, the plant-based diet is like a vegan diet where no animal products are involved. But the truth is that the person who is following a plant-based diet can consume chicken, meat, or fish occasionally. The main focus is on the whole and healthy food items rather than the processed items.

Why a Plant-Based Diet?

Why not? The health benefits associated with this diet make it one of the most highly recommended diet plans to follow.

The plant-based diet has very few restrictions, and it is not expensive to follow.
The meal plans are healthy, delicious, and good for your body.
The plant-based diet is high in fiber, water, and complex carbohydrates, which help the person to remain full for a longer period.
It is highly recommended for aged people, teenagers, nursing moms, and pregnant women.
A lot of research and evidence prove that it helps to lose weight effectively.
People who eat plant-based diets have low BMI, lower rates of heart disease, and lower cholesterol.
It is also effective in helping to prevent and manage diabetes.

Starting a Diet and Weight Loss

Starting a plant-based diet is easy: you do not need to eliminate huge food categories, and you do not need to subscribe to any expensive online plan. You need to follow these simple steps to get started with the diet plan:

Add more fruits and vegetables to your diet.

Start the day with a bowl of salad or soup.

Always cook a meal in oils that are plant-based like canola, olive oil, and peanut oil.

If you feel, need to munch on something, choose nuts and seeds for snacking.

For breakfast, choose tea and coffee that is unsweetened and without animal milk.

The meal should be comprised of those food items that are organic, whole, and full of vitamins, minerals, and protein.

You may add limited sweet treats. It's better to satisfy the sweet craving with fruit-based desserts and drinks.

It is highly recommended to only have 5-10% of the calories in your meal be from meat.

Try to include grain and legumes.

Choose your breakfast wisely by adding bread made with buckwheat, barley, or wheat.

"Go green" is the tagline for a vegan diet plan, and it is the best choice possible for healthy foods.

Advantages/benefits of Plant-Based Diet and Its Usefulness

Prevent hypertension

The addition of healthy green vegetables, fruits, and healthy unprocessed food items contribute toward low blood pressure. When a person switches to a plant-based diet, it automatically reduces the blood pressure and increases the potassium. The potassium helps in lowering hypertension and anxiety. The nuts, legume, and grains provide vitamin b6 that helps to lower the blood pressure.

Effective weight loss

Different research and study conduct that people following a plant-based diet tend to have a very low body mass index and have lower chances of getting obese. They also tend to have a very low rate of heart disease and diabetes. The plant-based diet plan is rich in fiber, protein, minerals, and calcium. All these nutrients make the body feel fuller for a longer period. It is one of the effective diets that treats obesity and reduces excess weight.

More energy and efficiency

The food groups that are part of the plant-based diet are rich in good fats and nutrients that provide instant energy to the body and cutting down the meat; you can reap a lot of health benefits.

Lower the rate of cancer and cardiovascular diseases.

The good fat and omega 3 rich food help lower the fat. The whole foods plant-based diet improves the chances of avoiding cancer as we cut on red meat, smoking, and alcohol, and we all know all these items are a link to increased heart diseases.

Chapter No 2: Create a Plant-Based Diet Using a Meal Plan

A plant-based diet means a lot of things rather than just one simple thing. It is not just a diet plan but a lifestyle to follow. So, whether you decided to cut out meat for animal welfare, want to lose weight, or just want to recover from or prevent illness like hypertension or diabetes, the plant-based diet is right for you. Following the plant-based diet using our meal plan is very simple; you just choose each day's meal before that day and fill your kitchen pantry with the necessary food items. Shopping ahead is a great way to save time. Arrange all the necessary cooking equipment before starting the cooking process and keep the cooking area clean.

The meal ideas that are suggested in the cookbook follow the plant-based diet premises and remove animal products and cheese completely. The recipe's directions are easy, and ingredients are readily available in markets and online grocery stores. This 21- day meal plan is the perfect way to get started on a plant-based diet.

Foods Allowed and Not Allowed

Food Allowed

- Fruits
- Vegetables: green leafy vegetables (e.g kale, spinach), carrots, parsnip, potatoes, squash, tomatoes, cauliflower, broccoli, etc.
- Whole grains
- Nuts butter
- Legumes
- Plant-based protein (tofu/tempeh)
- Nuts
- Seeds(flax seed. Chia seeds, pumpkin seeds, etc)
- Plant-based oils
- Spices and herbs
- Unsweetened coffee
- Unsweetened tea
- Unsweetened sparkling water

Food Not Allowed

- Fast food
- Candies
- Frozen food items
- Desserts

- Sweetened beverages
- Carbonated beverages
- Refined grains: white rice, white bread, refined pasta, etc.
- Packaged food items: cookies, chips, sugary cereals, etc.
- Processed meats: bacon, sausage, etc.

Stress Management and Mindset

When following a diet plan, a lot of questions arise about money and budget allocation and the time required. These things play a huge part in following a diet plan. The most stressful thing when starting any diet plan is to incorporate it into daily life. Food preferences, religious beliefs, health requirements, and medical needs make it harder to follow any diet plan. Therefore, we are giving some guidelines or tips that help anyone adapt to the 21-day challenge.

- Always fill half of the plate with salad or fruit.
- Stop drinking after and during the meal.
- Adjust timing to eat every meal at the same time; it helps stop feelings of food deprivation and unnecessary cravings. When the stomach is full, the body remains satisfied.

- Stay away from artificial sweetener and packed or processed food items
- Cut out junk food times.
- Always check food labels for any artificial or hidden sugar
- Go for seasonal fruits and vegetables and buy them from the local farmer's market.
- Try to cook a fresh meal.
- Emphasize whole-wheat grains and organic, fresh and seasonal vegetables and fruits
- Once the food in the fringe is consumed, go out to buy more.

Myths and Misconception About A Plant-Based Diet

It is an expensive diet plan. It is one of the most accessible diet plans with food choices that are not at all expensive, such as legumes, beans, and grains, which cost less than meat or fish.

The plant-based diet doesn't mean you become vegetarian or vegan. This diet allows you to enjoy meat, fish, poultry, and dairy in small amounts.

You need to skip some favorite snacks like ice-cream or candies. You do not need to skip any of your favorite snacks; they just need to be replaced with healthy alternatives such as a frozen fruit bar with no added or refined sugar.

The plant-based diet is bland and boring. This is not the case. It includes a wide variety of food items that no other diet offers. No big food group is being eliminated in his diet; it is just about setting limits, avoiding bad food choices, and going organic and all-natural.

It is not for people with kidney disease. This is not the case because the plant-based diet provides health benefits for people with kidney disease. A plant-based diet fits the basic needs of most of the people with a medical condition. Always ask your physician before starting a new diet.

Chapter 4: 21-Day Challenge and Beyond

The 21-days meal plan needs motivation and willpower for the proper mind-set to resist junk food items. On the other hand, it does not need complex planning or expenditure. The 21-day plan provides you with a schedule of what to prepare for the specific day. When you are heading to the market to buy the food, your plan should be clear so you can spend money effectively and save time as well.

If you continually stop just to check sale items, it's taking away your concentration and energy.

You need to make the following changes for 21 days:

- Write out your grocery list before you go shopping.
- Check the recipes you will be preparing for the next week and write down the things you need to buy.
- Make sure you buy enough to cover the meals you will prepare and serve.
- Buy fresh and best-quality products.
- Allow yourself sufficient time to prepare the meals for the week (or Three days at a minimum); it helps you to overcome any

frustration of not finishing things on time. The plan is full of versatile recipes that lack monotony.

Plant-Based v. Vegan v. Vegetarian

There are three types of diets that rely mainly or entirely on plants for nutrition:

Plant-Based – The diet consists mainly of whole plant foods, including fruit, vegetables, legumes, grains, nuts, and seeds. Dairy and other meat products are included in limited amounts. It avoids processed foods.

Vegan – Vegan is a lifestyle as well as a diet. The diet is entirely plant-based. The lifestyle is based on the protection of animal rights and stretches into clothing and skincare.

Vegetarian – The diet eliminates meat from the diet, but generally allows milk and eggs. Some vegetarian diets also include fish.

Pros and Cons of a Plant-Based Diet

Pros – The health benefits of a plant-based diet are supported by many years of research:

Improved heart health (e.g., lower blood pressure, lower heart rate, lower risk of heart attack/stroke).

Lower total cholesterol and "bad" LDL levels

Lower risk of developing type 2 diabetes and improvement of existing type 2 diabetes

Weight management

Protection against some types of cancer

Prevention and management of dementia and Alzheimer's Disease

Reduced carbon footprint

Cons – There is no doubt that transitioning to a plant-based diet is good for your health. However, there are a few issues that need to be kept in mind. You need to plan your meals carefully to make sure you do not suffer any of these side effects:

Low protein intake

Iron deficiency

Low intake of calcium and vitamin D leading to increased risk of bone fracture

Vitamin B12 deficiency

Lower essential fatty acid intake

Frequently Asked Questions

Q. Is this going to be expensive?

A. Not at all. Plant-based food (e.g., rice, beans, legumes, bananas, etc.) are a lot less expensive than meats and processed foods. You can buy dry bulk items to get even better prices. Farmers' markets are great produce and legume source in season, and you can buy frozen produce and canned beans at other times.

Can I get everything my body needs from plants?
A. Plants are full of vitamins, minerals, proteins, fats, and carbohydrates. They come from nature and are meant to be our food. You will be able to create well-balanced, nutritional meals in no time.

Q. Will I get enough protein?
A. Absolutely. Beans, nuts, and seeds are excellent sources of protein. In reality, almost all foods contain protein. For example, you can get protein from fruit, quinoa, black beans, and broccoli.

Q. Will I feel full eating only plants?
A. Yes. You will be eating a lot of fiber, and fiber makes you feel full. Natural foods provide the nutrients (e.g., vitamins and minerals) that your body needs, so it will feel satisfied. You may even find that you are eating more slowly to enjoy the different textures of the foods.
You will feel full, but you won't feel stuffed.

Q. Will I need dietary supplements?
A. Many authorities suggest taking Vitamin D, Vitamin B12, and Omega-3 supplements. You should check with your doctor before switching to any new

plan of eating, including moving to a plant-based diet. They will be able to tell you which supplement you will require.

Q. There any short-term side effects?
A. If you are not getting enough calories, you may experience fatigue and headaches. Additionally, a significant increase in the amount of fiber you eat will lead to increased bowel activity, so there may be some intestinal distress at the beginning. You may want to transition slowly to give your bowels time to adapt.

Chapter No: 5 21 Days Meal Plan Recipes (Total Recipes126)

The aim and motivation behind written this part of the book is to:

- Involve the whole family in cooking some healthy plant-based recipes
- Preparing the recipe with the tastiest ingredient available.
- Use all organic and natural food items to prepare a meal.

Along with recipes, nutritional information is also provided, as well. Listed below are some useful tips to start an effective cooking process.

- Use a clean stove and utensils
- Clean the kitchen before starting the actual cooking process
- Wash all the vegetables and fruits well before cooking
- Use heatproof spatula and skillet and cooking pot
- Always grease the baking pan for baking purposes.

Core Practices Good Habits

Good eating habits are crucial to be cultivated for an efficient living; this does not happen in a short period, so following this diet plan, the 21 days are enough to practice the following points:

- Learn the tactic to purchase effectively.
- Bypass all the artificial and processed food items
- Do not indulge in bad eating habits like junk or fast food.
- Eat meal on time
- Eat out from the same plate, so you know that what and how much you have eaten.
- Cook and prepare all the meals at home
- Eat vegetables and fruits of all color and seasons
- Do not throw any leftovers.
- Check the expiry dates of food item you purchased
- Once the fridge empties, then buy the next food items for next week or day.

Day 1

Breakfast

Orange French toast

It is a classic recipe of French toast with a twist of not so secret ingredients known as applesauce. These delicious and tasty French toasts are made with the addition of berries compote and plant-based bread made from whole-wheat flour.

Cooking Time: 14 Minutes
Yield: 4 Servings

Ingredients

Ingredients for French toast

2-1/2 cups of almond milk, unsweetened
1 cup of almond flour
2 cups of applesauce
4 tablespoons of maple syrup, pure
½ teaspoon of cinnamon powder
Salt
1 tablespoon of orange zest
12 whole-grain bread slices

Ingredients for Berry Compote

1 cup raspberries, fresh
1 cup applesauce
1 teaspoon of pure maple syrup

Directions

Preheat the oven to 400 degrees F.
Take a mixing bowl and mix almond milk, almond flour, maple syrup, cinnamon, salt, and applesauce.
Mix the ingredients well.
Transfer the mixture to any shallow pan and add orange zest to it.
Mix all the ingredients well.
Heat a non-stick skillet, and start dipping each bread piece into a pan mixture.
Soak for a few seconds, then place it in the skillet and cook over medium for 2 minutes per side.
Place the cooked toast on serving plate and bake in the oven for 10 minutes to make it crisper.
Now, make a berry compote.
Combine berries, applesauce, and maple syrup in a blender and pulse until smooth.
Server it with French toasts.
Enjoy.

Nutrition Facts
Servings: 4
Amount per serving
Calories   719
% Daily Value*
Total Fat 36.8g   47%
Saturated Fat 25.7g   128%
Cholesterol 0mg   0%
Sodium 426mg   19%
Total Carbohydrate 88.6g   32%
Dietary Fiber 13.8g   49%
Total Sugars 44.7g
Protein 14g

Lunch

Coconut Cauliflower Curry

A perfect stew with the authentic taste of curry that is beets served with steamed brown rice.
It is a very easy recipe that is prepared within 30 minutes.

Cooking Time: 25 Minutes
Yield: 6-8 Servings

Ingredients

1 yellow onion
1 pound sweet potato, chopped
1 head cauliflower, chopped
2 tablespoons olive oil
1 teaspoon of salt, divided
2 tablespoons curry powder
1 tablespoon Garam Masala
1 teaspoon cumin
¼ teaspoon cayenne
30ounces of diced tomatoes
15 ounces can full-fat coconut milk
15 ounces chickpeas
4 cups spinach leaves
Cilantro, for garnish

2 cups of brown rice, uncooked

Directions

The first step is to prepare the brown rice according to recipe needs.

Meanwhile, heat olive oil in a non-stick skillet and add onions to it.

Cook onions for 2 minutes, then add sweet potatoes and sauté for 3 minutes.

Next, add salt and cauliflower, cook for 5 minutes.

Add curry powder and Garam Masala, cumin, cayenne, and tomatoes.

Cook for 5 minutes and add coconut milk.

Simmer the mixture for 5 minutes and then add drained chickpeas and 4 cups of spinach

Stir it for 2 minutes and cook it until spinach is wilted.

Once cooked, serve over cooked, steamed rice.

Enjoy with a garnish of cilantro.

Nutrition Facts
Servings: 8
Amount per serving
Calories   627
% Daily Value*
Total Fat 23g   29%
Saturated Fat 13.8g   69%

Cholesterol 0mg 0%
Sodium 365mg 16%
Total Carbohydrate 92.3g 34%
Dietary Fiber 17.4g 62%
Total Sugars 15.7g
Protein 18.8g

Dinner

Dinnertime Vegetable Soup

This hearty and filling soup is the best alternative to any meal, and it is filled with the goodness of beets, carrots, and lentils. The touch of carrot juice makes it sweet, and the Brussels sprouts create uniqueness to this soup recipe.

Cooking Time: 50 Minutes
Yield: 4 Servings

Ingredients

6 cups organic vegetable broth
1 cup of water
1 onion, chopped
4 garlic cloves, chopped
1 beet peeled and chopped
2 cups Brussels sprouts, cut in half
2 cups carrot juice
1/3 cup green lentils, uncooked
1/4 cup red lentils, uncooked
1 cup kidney beans, organic
20 ounces of tomato sauce
1/3 teaspoon cinnamon
1/3 teaspoon Garam Masala

2 tablespoons of peanut butter
Sea salt and black pepper, to taste

Directions

Take a large cooking pot and add garlic, onions, and water in it.
Then add vegetable broth, and cook until wilted.
Add cinnamon powder and Garam Masala.
Adjust salt by taste.
Now, add chopped vegetables and sauté for 10 minutes.
Next, add red lentils, green lentils, carrot juice, beans, and tomato sauce.
Stir in the butter.
Simmer it for 30 minutes by covering with the lid.
Once the soup is ready, and ingredients are tender, serve.

Nutrition Facts
Servings: 4
Amount per serving
Calories   429
% Daily Value*
Total Fat 7.3g 9%
Saturated Fat 1.6g   8%
Cholesterol 0mg   0%
Sodium 2003mg   87%

Total Carbohydrate 65.8g   24%
Dietary Fiber 19g   68%
Total Sugars 16g
Protein 29.2g

Snack

Roasted Chickpeas

It is very easy to make and scrumptious snack recipe that is prepared quickly with fewer and inexpensive ingredients. The snack is full of nutrients. The taste of tamari and lemon goes well with chickpeas.

Cooking Time: 20 Minutes
Yield: 3 Servings

Ingredients

16 ounces of chick peas, drained and rinsed
2 teaspoons of olive oil
2 teaspoons of lemon juice, freshly squeezed
2 tablespoons of tamari sauce
Salt, pinch
¼ cup of agave nectar

Directions

Preheat the oven to 420 degrees F.
Layer the baking sheet with parchment paper.
In a bowl, add all the ingredients and toss well.
And layer the chickpeas on a baking sheet.
Bake in oven utile chickpea absorbs the ingredients.

Serve at room temperature.

Nutrition Facts
Servings: 3
Amount per serving
Calories   220
% Daily Value*
Total Fat 4.9g 6%
Saturated Fat 0.7g   3%
Cholesterol 0mg   0%
Sodium 1173mg   51%
Total Carbohydrate 36.3g   13%
Dietary Fiber 6.8g   24%
Total Sugars 1.5g
Protein 8.8g

Drink /Smoothie

Tropical Smoothie

It is a perfect tropical smoothie recipe that is full of nutrients because it includes apple, spinach, ginger, pineapple, and other healthy ingredients. It is a 100 perfect plant-based recipe with only natural sweetness.

Cooking Time: 0 Minutes
Yield: 4 Servings

Ingredients

1 apple, cut into pieces
1 cup pineapple, chunks
1-inch ginger, peeled and chopped
1 cup baby spinach
2 bananas
1-1/2 cup of coconut milk
Pinch of sea salt
¼ cup of water
1 teaspoon of hemp seed

Directions

Take a high-speed blender and put coconut milk, water, apple, ginger, baby spinach, banana, salt, pineapple, water, and hemp seed in it.
Pulse it for 2 minutes.
Then add ice-cubes and pulse for 30 more seconds.
Pour into serving glasses and enjoy chilled.

Nutrition Facts
Servings: 4
Amount per serving
Calories   264
% Daily Value*
Total Fat 16.4g   21%
Saturated Fat 12.9g   64%
Cholesterol 0mg   0%
Sodium 76mg 3%
Total Carbohydrate 30.8g   11%
Dietary Fiber 5.1g   18%
Total Sugars 19.1g
Protein 3.9g

Dessert

Double Chocolate Cupcakes

It is a very delicious and easy to make cupcakes that are dessert time hit. The addition of dates makes it extremely fudgy.

Cooking Time: 25 Minutes
Yield: 4 Servings

Ingredients

2.5 ounces chocolate, nondairy and unsweetened
1-1/2 cups unsweetened almond milk
1 teaspoon apple cider vinegar
⅔ Cup dry maple sugar
1/3 cup unsweetened applesauce
½ teaspoon pure vanilla extract
1-1/2 cups spelt flour
1/3 cup cocoa powder, unsweetened
1/4 teaspoon baking soda
1 teaspoon baking powder
Salt, pinch

Directions

Preheat the oven to 375 degrees F.

Line a muffin tray with muffin cups.

In a bowl melt chocolate, using the microwave.

Set it aside.

Take a large bowl and combine milk and apple cider vinegar.

Set aside for a few minutes.

Once curdled, add maple sugar, vanilla, chocolate, and applesauce.

Take a separate bowl ad to add flour, baking soda, cocoa powder, baking powder, and salt.

Add wet ingredients into the dry ingredients and combine ingredients of both the bowls.

Mix until no lump remains.

Scoop this batter to the muffins tray.

Bake for 25 minutes.

Remove the muffins afterward and put them on a cooling rack.

Serve and enjoy.

Nutrition Facts

Servings: 4

Amount per serving

Calories 319

% Daily Value*

Total Fat 7.7g 10%

Saturated Fat 4.4g 22%

Cholesterol 4mg 1%

Sodium 184mg 8%

Total Carbohydrate 61.5g 22%

Dietary Fiber 6.9g   25%
Total Sugars 31.9g
Protein 7.1g

Day 2

Breakfast

Chocolate Chip Coconut Pancakes

These are simple yet scrumptious pancakes that are made with some finest ingredients. We used a griddle to cook these pancakes to perfection just in few minutes. The pancakes are not only satisfied but also provide all the nutrition that we need to kick start the hectic routine.

Cooking Time: 10 Minutes
Yield: 4 Servings

Ingredients

2 tablespoons of flaxseed
1-1/2 cups of buckwheat flour
1/3 cup old-fashioned rolled oats
3 tablespoons unsweetened coconut flakes
½ tablespoon baking powder
Pinch of salt
1 cup unsweetened almond milk
1/3 cup unsweetened applesauce
1/3 cup pure maple syrup
1 teaspoon pure vanilla extract

⅓ Cup chocolate chips, unsweetened

Directions

Pour water about ½ cup in a bowl and add flax seeds to it.
Cook the flax seeds over medium heat.
Once the mixture gets thick, strain the flax seeds mixture into a cup and set aside.
Discard the seeds.
Take a mixing bowl and mix buckwheat, oats, coconut flakes, baking powder, and salt,
In a medium bowl, mix together applesauce, milk, maple syrup, vanilla, and reserved flaxseed water.
Mix dry mixture to liquid mixture.
Now, stir in the chocolate chip.
Now, heat a griddle over the medium heat and pour the batter of pancake on to the griddle.
Cook for 5 minutes.
Once, the bubble form on top cook from the other side.
Once done, repeat with the remaining mixture.
Then serve and enjoy.

Nutrition Facts
Servings: 4
Amount per serving
Calories   303

% Daily Value*
Total Fat 7.8g 10%
Saturated Fat 3.8g   19%
Cholesterol 3mg   1%
Sodium 104mg   5%
Total Carbohydrate 54.4g   20%
Dietary Fiber 5.4g   19%
Total Sugars 26g
Protein 6.3g

Lunch

Healthy Green Soup

It is one of the likable soups to enjoy as a lunch.

Cooking Time: 20 Minutes
Yield: 4 Servings

Ingredients

½ cups broccoli
6 cups vegetable broth, unsalted
1 cup of water
½ cup cauliflower florets
1 cup Bok Choy
2 teaspoons lemon juice
2 teaspoons five-spice powder
6 ounces of Snow peas, trimmed
Salt and black pepper, to taste

Directions

Place all the ingredients in the instant pot and lock the lid.
Set timer to 20 minutes at high.
Once the timer beeps, release the steam naturally.

Now transfer the soup to the blender and pulse it for a few minutes.
Before serving, re-heat it.
Serve and enjoy.

Nutrition Facts
Servings: 4
Amount per serving
Calories   88
% Daily Value*
Total Fat 2.3g 3%
Saturated Fat 0.6g   3%
Cholesterol 0mg   0%
Sodium 1168mg   51%
Total Carbohydrate 6.4g   2%
Dietary Fiber 2.3g   8%
Total Sugars 3.5g
Protein 9.7g

Dinner

Tacos with Salsa

It is a very healthy and hearty recipe to enjoy that is full of nutrients.

Cooking Time: 10Minutes
Yield: 4 Servings

Ingredients

30 ounces of pinto beans, rinsed and drained
4 tablespoons of Dijon mustard
2 teaspoon of maple syrup
½ cup ketchup
1 teaspoon of garlic
¼ teaspoon chili powder
Salt, to taste
2 cups of pineapple chunks
1/3 cup minced red onion
1/4 cup finely chopped cilantro
½ small green cabbage, sliced
4 radishes, sliced
1 lime, sliced
12 Tortillas, for serving

Directions

Drain and rinse the beans.
Take a skillet and put the beans, mustard, ketchup, maple syrup, garlic powder, chili powder, salt, and garlic powder in it.
Heat it over low heat.
Mix pineapple, red onions, and cilantro in a bowl and add salt to it.
Now slice the cabbage and radish along with lime.
Now start making tortilla by placing it over gas flame over medium for few seconds.
Next, place the beans, cabbage, radish in a tortilla, and end with a squeeze of lime.
Top it off with pineapple salsa.
Serve and enjoy.

Nutrition Facts
Servings: 4
Amount per serving
Calories   1018
% Daily Value*
Total Fat 5.7g 7%
Saturated Fat 0.9g   5%
Cholesterol 0mg   0%
Sodium 630mg   27%
Total Carbohydrate 194.9g   71%
Dietary Fiber 42.3g   151%

Total Sugars 25.8g
Protein 52.8g

Snack

Gluten-Free Pistachios

It is a perfect treat for all pistachio lovers.

Cooking Time: 20minutes
Yield: 4 Servings

Ingredients

2 cups pistachios, shelled and salted
2 tablespoons of pure maple syrup
½ teaspoon of ginger, powdered

Directions

Preheat the oven to 300 degrees F.
Take a bowl and mix ginger and pistachio in it.
Pour maple syrup on top.
Stir well for fine coating.
Layer the pistachio on a baking dish lined with parchment paper.
Bake it in the oven for 20 minutes.
Once nuts are crisp, take out from the oven and let it sit for cooling.
Serve and enjoy.

Nutrition Facts
Servings: 4
Amount per serving
Calories 187
% Daily Value*
Total Fat 14g 18%
Saturated Fat 1.5g 8%
Cholesterol 0mg 0%
Sodium 161mg 7%
Total Carbohydrate 14.9g 5%
Dietary Fiber 3g 11%
Total Sugars 8g
Protein 6g

Drink/Smoothie

Avocado Banana Smoothie

If you want to enjoy a perfect sip of flavors and taste then this recipe is for you.

Cooking Time: 0 Minutes
Yield: 4 Servings

Ingredients

1 large banana, frozen
1 large avocado, ripped
1 scoop of plant-based vanilla protein powder
1 cup baby spinach, chopped
1 cup kale
2 cups almond milk, unsweetened
1 tablespoon of hemp seed
1 teaspoon of flaxseed
1/2 cup organic berries, frozen

Directions

Add bananas, protein powder, and avocado, greens, and almond milk in a high-speed blender.
Next, add hemp seed, flaxseed, and berries.
Blend until smooth in the paste.

Pour the smoothie into ice-filled serving glasses. Once it's chilled, serve.

Nutrition Facts
Servings: 4
Amount per serving
Calories   483
% Daily Value*
Total Fat 41g 53%
Saturated Fat 27.6g   138%
Cholesterol 0mg   0%
Sodium 132mg   6%
Total Carbohydrate 24.3g   9%
Dietary Fiber 8.2g   29%
Total Sugars 9.7g
Protein 11.5g

Dessert

Lemony Oats Cookies

These are chewy and most delicious cookies that are baked for 35 minutes to its perfection.

Cooking Time: 35 Minutes
Yield: 4 Servings

Ingredients

12 dates, pitted
1/3 cup unsweetened applesauce
2 teaspoons apple cider vinegar
1-1/2 cup rolled oats
1 cup oat flour
¼ cup quick-cooking oats
½ cup roughly chopped walnuts
1 tablespoon lemon zest
4 teaspoons cocoa powder, natural
1 teaspoon vanilla powder
1 teaspoon baking soda
Salt, pinch

Directions

Preheat the oven to 300 degrees F.

Line a baking sheet with parchment paper.

Take a bowl, and add dates and cover it with hot water

Let the dates soak for one hour.

Drain the water and take out the date.

Transfer the dates to a blender and add applesauce, vinegar, and blend.

Set aside the paste.

Take a separate bowl and add oats, flour, and quick-cooking oats, lemon zest, walnuts, vanilla powder, baking soda, salt, and cocoa powder.

Add the date mix to the flour mixture.

Mix well.

Use a wooden spatula to mix the ingredients.

Scoop a golf-sized ball of batter on to the flat surface and flatten with hands.

Place these cookies onto a baking pan.

Bake in the oven for 35 minutes.

Once, cooked transfer it to the baking rack and let it get cool at room temperature.

Once, it's done serve.

Nutrition Facts
Servings: 4
Amount per serving
Calories   305
% Daily Value*
Total Fat 5.6g 7%

Saturated Fat 1g 5%
Cholesterol 0mg 0%
Sodium 444mg 19%
Total Carbohydrate 59.3g 22%
Dietary Fiber 7.6g 27%
Total Sugars 23g
Protein 7.5g

Day 3

Breakfast

Eggless Scrambles

The tofu adds richness, and it is a best alternative to egg scramble.

Cooking Time: 20minutes
Yield: 2 Servings

Ingredients

1 green onion, chopped
1-1/2 cup firm raw tofu, drained
1 small red tomatoes, chopped
½ teaspoon of turmeric
½ teaspoon of cumin
2 teaspoons of lemon juice
4 slices of Rye Bread, toasted
2 tablespoons of olive oil
½ teaspoon of sesame seeds
Salt and black pepper, to taste

Directions

Pour oil to a nonstick skillet.

Now, add green onions to the pan.
Once, sizzling add tomatoes, lemon juice, cumin, sesame seeds, and turmeric.
Now add tofu and make a scramble in pan.
Adjust seasoning by adding salt and black pepper.
Avoid overcooking and making it a mush.
Now toast the bread and place a generous amount of scramble over bread slices.
Serve and enjoy hot.

Nutrition Facts
Servings: 2
Amount per serving
Calories   265
% Daily Value*
Total Fat 20.4g   26%
Saturated Fat 3.3g   17%
Cholesterol 0mg   0%
Sodium 113mg   5%
Total Carbohydrate 12.1g   4%
Dietary Fiber 3g   11%
Total Sugars 2.8g
Protein 12.4g

Lunch

Simple Veggies Stew

As by name it is a simple and classic veggie stew recipes to enjoy at lunch.

Cooking Time: 35 Minutes
Yield: 4 Servings

Ingredients

2 green zucchinis, chopped
½ tablespoon garlic powder
2 cups of water
½ cup turnip, peeled and chopped
2 cups of coconut milk
Salt, to taste
Black pepper, to taste
½ cup Swiss chard, chopped
½ cup spinach stems removed
½ cup Brussels sprout

Directions

Pour water in a cooking pan and let it boil over medium heat.

Now add zucchini, turnip, Swiss chard, spinach, and Brussels sprouts in the water and cook for 15 minutes covered.
Now, add garlic powder, salt, and black pepper.
Simmer for 5 minutes and add coconuts milk.
Let it cook it for 12 more minutes, covered.
Once done, serve the stew.
Enjoy.

Nutrition Facts
Servings: 4
Amount per serving
Calories   301
% Daily Value*
Total Fat 28.7g   37%
Saturated Fat 25.4g   127%
Cholesterol 0mg   0%
Sodium 87mg 4%
Total Carbohydrate 11.8g   4%
Dietary Fiber 4.6g   16%
Total Sugars 6.2g
Protein 4.1g

Dinner

Green Gram Split Lentil Recipe

It is a perfect plant based recipes rich in mineral protein and vitamins.

Cooking Time: 35 Minutes
Yield: 2 Servings

Ingredients

1 cup of green gram split, pre-soaked (without skin)
4 cups of water
2 garlic cloves, paste
½ teaspoon of ginger, paste
Salt, to taste
1 teaspoon organic coriander Powder
1/4 teaspoon organic turmeric Powder
4 teaspoons of Olive oil
2 small red onions, chopped
1teaspoon Organic Cumin
¼ teaspoon of red chili powder
2 green chilies, chopped

Directions

Soak the lentil for 40 minutes, before starting the cooking.
Drain the lentils and set aside.
In a large cooking pot, add water, lentil, salt, onions, lentils, coriander powder, turmeric powder, chili powder, and cumin powder.
Bring it to boil and cook for 30 minutes covered.
Next, take a medium skillet and pour olive oil.
Add garlic and ginger paste to it.
Cook until lightly brown.
Pour this mixture over the lentil.
Mix the lentil, and then serve with green chilli garnish if liked.

Nutrition Facts
Servings: 2
Amount per serving
Calories   197
% Daily Value*
Total Fat 10.3g   13%
Saturated Fat 1.4g   7%
Cholesterol 0mg   0%
Sodium 103mg   4%
Total Carbohydrate 22.5g   8%
Dietary Fiber 5.6g   20%

Total Sugars 3.8g
Protein 6.3g

Snack

Cauliflower Poppers with Sauce

It is a delicious popper recipe to enjoy as a snack.

Cooking Time: 24 Hours
Yield: 6 Servings

Ingredients

2 heads of cauliflower, florets

Ingredients For Sauce

1 cup dates, pitted
½ cup of filtered water
½ cup sun-dried tomatoes
2 tablespoons nutritional yeast
4 tablespoons raw tahini
2 tablespoons apple cider vinegar
1 teaspoon cayenne pepper
1 teaspoon garlic powder
1 teaspoon onion powder
1 teaspoon turmeric

Directions

First, chop the cauliflower into bite-size pieces.
Next, take a high-speed blender and add all the sauce ingredients in it.
Blend until reaching a thick consistency.
Pour the sauce over cauliflower.
Toss the florets well for fine coating.
Place the florets onto your dehydrator trays.
Dehydrate at 115 F for 12 - 24 hours.
Once desire crunchiness reaches serve and enjoy.

Nutrition Facts
Servings: 6
Amount per serving
Calories   164
% Daily Value*
Total Fat 5.8g 7%
Saturated Fat 0.8g   4%
Cholesterol 0mg   0%
Sodium 16mg 1%
Total Carbohydrate 27.6g   10%
Dietary Fiber 4.6g   16%
Total Sugars 19.6g
Protein 4.3g

Drink/Smoothie

Blueberry, And Almond Butter Smoothie

It is a very creamy, rich, and thick smoothie that is busting with great flavors and taste amazing. It is not only a scrumptious smoothie but also packed with protein.

Cooking Time: 0 Minutes
Yield: 2 Servings

Ingredients

2 cups of ripe bananas
1 cup blueberries, frozen
2 tablespoons of almond butter
1 cup almond milk
1 tablespoon flaxseed meal
1 teaspoon of chia seed
2 tablespoons of protein powder

Directions

Take a high-speed blender and put all the ingredients in it.
Pulse it for few seconds and pour it into ice-filled serving glasses.

Serve and enjoy.

Nutrition Facts
Servings: 2
Amount per serving
Calories   645
% Daily Value*
Total Fat 41.5g   53%
Saturated Fat 27g   135%
Cholesterol 32mg   11%
Sodium 50mg 2%
Total Carbohydrate 58.8g   21%
Dietary Fiber 12.1g   43%
Total Sugars 30.8g
Protein 20.7g

Dessert

Raspberry Brownies

It is a mouth-watering, fudgy, and creamy brownie, rich with the taste and texture that melts in your mouth. The blueberries add extra taste and antioxidant qualities.

Cooking Time: 20 Minutes
Yield: 4 Servings

Ingredients

1 cup raspberry jam, organic and all-natural
6 ounces of chocolate, unsweetened and chopped
1 cup of cane sugar
1 cup of applesauce
1 teaspoon of vanilla extract
¼ teaspoon almond extract
2 cups whole wheat pastry flour
1/3 cup unsweetened cocoa powder
1 teaspoon baking powder
1 teaspoon baking soda
1/6 teaspoon salt
½ cup raspberries, frozen

Directions

Preheat the oven to 375 degrees F.
Line a baking sheet over a baking pan.
Take a bowl and melt chocolate in it by placing it in the microwave, for a few seconds.
Take a large bowl and mix applesauce, jam, sweetener, vanilla, also extract and melted chocolate
Mix it very well.
Now stir in flour, baking powder, baking soda, salt, and cocoa powder.
At the end folds in the raspberries
Mix well and spread the mixture into the baking pan lined with parchment paper.
Bake it in the oven for 20 minutes.
Once done remove it from the oven and let it sit on the cooling rack.
Once it's cool, serve by slicing in to brownie shapes.

Nutrition Facts
Servings: 4
Amount per serving
Calories   707
% Daily Value*
Total Fat 14.7g   19%
Saturated Fat 9.4g   47%
Cholesterol 10mg   3%
Sodium 498mg   22%

Total Carbohydrate 135.6g 49%
Dietary Fiber 11.6g 41%
Total Sugars 66g
Protein 11.3g

Day 4

Breakfast

Breakfast Blueberries Pancakes

This recipe is rich with the antioxidant qualities of blueberries.

Cooking Time: 22 Minutes
Yield: 3 Servings

Ingredients

2 cups spelt flour
1 scoop stevia
2 eggs
1-1/4 cup cashew milk, unsweetened
½ cup blueberries, fresh and chopped
½ cup strawberries, fresh and chopped
1 cup almonds flour
Oil spray for greasing

Directions

Mix spelt flour and almond flour in a large bowl.
Pour milk in the flour and mix well.
Add 2 eggs and combine ingredients.

Stir the ingredients to make a runny consistency.
Make sure no lump remains.
In the end, add stevia and chopped berries.
If the consistency is too watery, then add a bit of more almond flour.
Grease a skillet or griddle with oil spray.
Pour the spoon full of the mixture to the griddle.
Once the bubbles formed on the top, flip to cook from another side.
Serve and enjoy.

Nutrition Facts
Servings: 3
Amount per serving
Calories   275
% Daily Value*
Total Fat 13g   17%
Saturated Fat 0.7g   3%
Cholesterol 0mg   0%
Sodium 228mg   10%
Total Carbohydrate 31.1g   11%
Dietary Fiber 5.3g   19%
Total Sugars 7.2g
Protein 7.2g

Lunch

Garlic Pasta

It is rich and creamy pasta infused with the taste of garlic and roasted tomatoes. The addition of almond flour makes it full of nutrition. It is a perfect plant-based recipe.

Cooking Time: 25 Minutes
Yield: 3 Servings

Ingredients

2 cups of tomatoes, cut in half
12 ounces of whole wheat pasta, penne
2 tablespoons of olive oil
4 shallots, chopped
6 cloves of garlic
Salt and black pepper, to taste
6 tablespoons of almond flour
6 tablespoons of almond milk
3 cups of vegetable stock, unsweetened

Directions

Preheat the oven at 420 degrees F.

Toss the tomatoes in sea salt, black pepper, and 1 tablespoon of olive oil.

Place the tomatoes on to the baking sheet lined with parchment paper.

Bake it in the oven for 20 minutes.

Meanwhile, prepare pasta by bringing water to boil in a large pot.

Cook pasta, according to package instruction.

Meanwhile, in a medium skillet, add remaining olive oil, garlic, almond flour, and shallots.

Add salt and black pepper.

Cook it for 2 minutes.

Add in almond milk little at a time so, there no lump remains.

Then, add in the stock.

Simmer and cook for 10 minutes.

Once the sauce is done, add the drained pasta to the sauce.

Add roasted tomatoes on top.

Garish it with the fresh basil.

Serve and enjoy.

Nutrition Facts

Servings: 3

Amount per serving

Calories   693

% Daily Value*

Total Fat 26.8g   34%

Saturated Fat 8.2g   41%

Cholesterol 0mg 0%
Sodium 83mg 4%
Total Carbohydrate 98.1g 36%
Dietary Fiber 14.2g 51%
Total Sugars 9.4g
Protein 19.8g

Dinner

Roasted Cauliflower Soup

It is a bowl of perfectly creamy and rich soup. Once, you sip it your mouth with bust with the delicious roasted flavor of cauliflower along with very aromatic and earthy flavors.

Cooking Time: 50 Minutes
Yield: 6-8 Servings

Ingredients

4 pounds of cauliflower florets, chopped
1.5 cups leeks, chopped
1 cup olive oil
Salt and black pepper, to taste
½ cup parsley
1 cup chives, chopped
10 cups of vegetable broth, unsalted and unsweetened
5 teaspoons of white wine vinegar

Directions

Preheat the oven to 375 degrees F.
Grease a baking sheet with oil.

In a bowl, place leeks and cauliflower, and toss it with salt, black pepper, and 1 tablespoon of olive oil.

Layer the vegetables in a baking sheet and bake for 30 minutes.

Meanwhile, blend the chives, parsley, salt, and black pepper to the paste.

Mix and add the remaining olive oil to the blender.

Take out the roasted vegetable from the oven and add to the pot.

Pour broth into the pot and bring the mixture to boil. Simmer it for 15 minutes.

Add in the white wine vinegar and cook for 5 minutes.

Then puree the mixture using a blender in batches.

In the end, stir in the herb sauce or swirl it on top.

Enjoy the soup hot.

Nutrition Facts

Servings: 8

Amount per serving

Calories 335

% Daily Value*

Total Fat 27.3g 35%

Saturated Fat 4.1g 21%

Cholesterol 0mg 0%

Sodium 1028mg 45%

Total Carbohydrate 16.1g 6%

Dietary Fiber 6.2g 22%

Total Sugars 7.1g
Protein 11.1

Snack

Banana-Oat Protein Balls

It is very easy to make three ingredients recipe that is filled with nutrients and packages with the power of super food, like a banana.

Cooking Time: 0 Minutes
Yield: 4 Servings

Ingredients

1-1/2 cup rolled oats
1 scoop of protein powder
2 large bananas, ripe

Directions

Place oats, protein powder, and banana in a food processor.
Pulse it until smooth.
Roll into 12 balls.
Place in a reusable container or serve immediately.

Nutrition Facts
Servings: 4
Amount per serving
Calories   168
% Daily Value*
Total Fat 2g   3%
Saturated Fat 0.5g   3%
Cholesterol 16mg   5%
Sodium 16mg 1%
Total Carbohydrate 30.3g   11%
Dietary Fiber 3.8g   14%
Total Sugars 8.8g
Protein 9g

Drink/Smoothie

Beets and Berry Smoothie

It is a very creamy smoothie, which is made with a combination of fruit and vegetables. The beets can be boiled and then added to the smoothie as well.

Cooking Time: 0 Minutes
Yield: 3 Servings

Ingredients

2 Clementine's, broken into segments
2 small beet, peeled and chopped
1 cup strawberries
2 bananas, preferably frozen
2 teaspoons of almond butter
1 cup unsweetened almond milk
Pinch of sea salt
Ice cubes for chilling

Directions

Dump all the listed ingredients in a high-speed blender and pulse into a smooth consistency.
Pour into a high-speed blender and serve chilled.
Enjoy.

Nutrition Facts
Servings: 3
Amount per serving
Calories 212
% Daily Value*
Total Fat 7.8g 10%
Saturated Fat 0.7g 3%
Cholesterol 0mg 0%
Sodium 184mg 8%
Total Carbohydrate 35g 13%
Dietary Fiber 6.7g 24%
Total Sugars 20.8g
Protein 5g

Dessert

Plant-Based Mug Cake

It is a simple cake that's made using mug in microwave using simple ingredients.

Cooking Time: 2 Minutes
Yield: 1 Serving

Ingredients

6 tablespoons of spelt flour
5 tablespoon of cocoa powder
1 scoop stevia
4 teaspoons of pumpkin puree
6 tablespoons cashew milk, unsweetened

Directions

Take a large microwave-safe mug and mix all the ingredients in it.
Mix until smooth texture obtained.
Place it in the microwave and cook for 2 minutes at a high temperature.
Once done, serve.

Nutrition Facts
Servings: 1
Amount per serving
Calories 273
% Daily Value*
Total Fat 6.6g 8%
Saturated Fat 2.1g 11%
Cholesterol 0mg 0%
Sodium 51mg 2%
Total Carbohydrate 53.4g 19%
Dietary Fiber 14.1g 50%
Total Sugars 1.1g
Protein 10.9g

Day 5

Breakfast

Panini Recipe

It is a very delicious and classic turn to a normal breakfast sandwich with the addition of peanut butter and chocolate. It is a plant-based and kid-friendly meal to enjoy in the early morning. This meal is rich in fiber, mineral, antioxidants, and potassium.

Cooking Time: 0 Minutes
Yield: 2 Servings

Ingredients

½ cup of raisins
½ cup of hot water
½ tablespoon cinnamon
4 teaspoons cacao powder
1/3 cup of natural peanut butter
2 ripe bananas
4 slices of whole-grain bread

Directions

Combine raisins, hot water, cacao powder, and cinnamon in a bowl.
Take whole grain bread, and put butter on it.
Slice the bananas, and layer on bread.
Blend raisin mixture in a blender and spread over bread.
Serve.

Nutrition Facts
Servings: 2
Amount per serving
Calories 723
% Daily Value*
Total Fat 31.8g 41%
Saturated Fat 9.6g 48%
Cholesterol 0mg 0%
Sodium 279mg 12%
Total Carbohydrate 108.1g 39%
Dietary Fiber 23.8g 85%
Total Sugars 41.7g
Protein 31.1g

Lunch

Quinoa Lime Burrito Bowl

It is a very light and low calories bowl to enjoy at lunch time.

Cooking Time: 20 Minutes
Yield: 2 Servings

Ingredient

2 cups quinoa
4 cups of water
1 teaspoon of chili powder
Salt, to taste
2 potatoes, cubed
2 cups black beans
3 cloves garlic, minced
1 small onion, diced
½ bell pepper, diced
1 cup cherry tomatoes
½ cup of cabbage
2 cups of baby spinach
2 avocados, sliced
2 limes, juiced
½ cup olive oil

Directions

Boil water in a cooking pot and cook quinoa in it for 15 minutes.
Once, the quinoa gets fluffy and cooked add chili powder, and lime juice in it
Mix well, and let it sit for a while for further use.
Peel the potatoes, and toss in olive oil.
Season it with salt and roast in the oven for 20 minutes.
Meanwhile, mix beans with garlic and heat in oven ro10 minutes.
In a mixing bowl, mix lime juice, salt, and olive oil.
Now, divide the beans, quinoa, and potatoes among two bowls, and top with bell pepper, onions, cabbage, baby spinach, and tomatoes.
Garnish it with the avocado slices.
Adjust the seasoning and serve.
Enjoy.

Nutrition Facts
Servings: 2
Amount per serving
Calories   2338
% Daily Value*
Total Fat 103.5g   133%
Saturated Fat 17.5g   88%
Cholesterol 0mg   0%

Sodium 183mg 8%
Total Carbohydrate 294.2g 107%
Dietary Fiber 63.8g 228%
Total Sugars 13.8g
Protein 76.3g

Dinner

Rosemary Balsamic Roasted Vegetable

It is a very light, hearty, and easy to make low calories dinner time vegetables. You can also add any other vegetable of your own choice. the rosemary makes it a very aromatic dish to enjoy.

Cooking Time: 35 Minutes
Yield: 2 Servings

Ingredients

1 pound of Brussels sprouts
½ medium cauliflower, florets
2 carrots, chopped
2 turnips, chopped and peeled
2 beets, peeled and chopped
2 sweet potatoes, peeled and chopped
3 tablespoons of balsamic vinegar
4 teaspoons of olive oil
2 teaspoons of honey
2 teaspoons of chopped rosemary
4 garlic cloves
1 teaspoon of onion powder
Salt and black pepper, to taste

Directions

Preheat the oven to 400 degrees F.
Line the baking sheet with parchment paper.
Spray oil on parchment paper.
Take a bowl and combine all the vegetables along with olive oil, balsamic vinegar, honey, rosemary, garlic cloves, onion powder, salt, and black pepper.
Toss all the ingredients well.
Place the vegetable on parchment paper.
Bake in the oven for 35 minutes.
Once vegetable gets tender, take out from the oven and serve.

Nutrition Facts
Servings: 2
Amount per serving
Calories   519
% Daily Value*
Total Fat 10.8g   14%
Saturated Fat 1.8g   9%
Cholesterol 0mg   0%
Sodium 293mg   13%
Total Carbohydrate 99.6g   36%
Dietary Fiber 22.6g   81%
Total Sugars 29.5g
Protein 15.1g

Snack

Dark Chocolate Figs

These are very delicious chocolate-covered figs that are healthy and nutritious snacks to enjoy.

Cooking Time: 0 Minutes
Yield: 4 Servings

Ingredients

1 cup chocolate, dark chocolate 100% cacao
16 fresh figs
1 cup raw walnuts, chopped

Directions

Put the chocolate in a microwave-safe bowl and melt in the microwave for a few seconds.
Dip the figs into melted chocolate.
Now place fig on parchment paper and sprinkle walnuts on top.
Refrigerate for 20 minutes, once solid serve.

Nutrition Facts
Servings: 4
Amount per serving

Calories 607
% Daily Value*
Total Fat 31.6g 41%
Saturated Fat 9.9g 49%
Cholesterol 10mg 3%
Sodium 41mg 2%
Total Carbohydrate 76.6g 28%
Dietary Fiber 11g 39%
Total Sugars 58.4g
Protein 13.2g

Drink/Smoothie

Smoothie Bowl

It is a very innovated and delicious bowl that can be enjoyed any time of day

Cooking Time: 0 Minutes
Yield: 4 Servings

Ingredients

1 avocado, frozen and pitted
2 bananas, frozen and sliced
½ cup blueberries, frozen
½ cup spinach, frozen
2 tablespoons maple syrup
1-1/2 cups of coconut milk

Topping Ingredients For A Smoothie

2 teaspoons of flaxseed meal
2 tablespoons of almond butter
½ teaspoon of sunflower seed
¼ cup shredded coconut

Directions

Dump avocado, bananas, blueberries, spinach, and maple syrup in a blender and pour coconut milk.
Blend for few seconds until smooth.
Add ice cubes and blend again for a fine consistency.
Pour into a large bowl and then top it with flax seed, almond butter, sunflower seed, and shredded coconut.
Serve and enjoy.

Nutrition Facts
Servings: 4
Amount per serving
Calories 404
% Daily Value*
Total Fat 31g 40%
Saturated Fat 16.7g 84%
Cholesterol 0mg 0%
Sodium 18mg 1%
Total Carbohydrate 33.2g 12%
Dietary Fiber 8.3g 30%
Total Sugars 17.9g
Protein 5.3g

Dessert

Quinoa Pudding

It is twist to pudding as we have added quinoa to make it healthier.

Cooking Time: 18 Minutes
Yield: 2 Servings

Ingredients

1 cup quinoa, pre-soaked
1 cup almond milk
3 cups of water
1 scoop of stevia
½ cup cashew cream, unsweetened

Directions

Boil water in a large cooking pot.
Add quinoa and cook for 15 minutes.
In a separate pan boil milk and add it to cooked quinoa.
At the end add cashew cream and stevia.
Mix it and pour in a serving bowl.
Refrigerate for few hours then serve.
Enjoy.

Nutrition Facts
Servings: 2
Amount per serving
Calories 654
% Daily Value*
Total Fat 37.5g 48%
Saturated Fat 28.2g 141%
Cholesterol 11mg 4%
Sodium 59mg 3%
Total Carbohydrate 68.2g 25%
Dietary Fiber 8.6g 31%
Total Sugars 9.8g
Protein 15.8g

Day 6

Breakfast

Mushroom, Olives and Chickpea Omelette

It is the best alternative to egg omelet, as well as very easy to make the recipe.

Cooking Time: 20 Minutes
Yield: 2 Servings

Ingredients

½ cup of chickpea flour
1 teaspoon of chopped onions
1 teaspoon of garlic minced
Salt and black pepper, to taste
1/3 nutritional yeast
1 teaspoon of baking soda
5 ounces sautéed mushrooms
2 ounces black olives, chopped
1 cup salsa

Directions

In a large mixing bowl add chickpea flour, onions, garlic, salt, black pepper, nutritional yeast, baking soda.
Add about 1 cup of water to make a smooth paste.
Heat olive oil in a frying pan and pour the batter into the pan.
Sprinkle mushrooms and black olives over the batter.
Once cooked from the bottom flip to cook for another side.
Serve it with the topping of salsa.
Enjoy hot.

Nutrition Facts
Servings: 2
Amount per serving
Calories   271
% Daily Value*
Total Fat 6.5g 8%
Saturated Fat 0.8g   4%
Cholesterol 0mg   0%
Sodium 1673mg   73%
Total Carbohydrate 43.7g   16%
Dietary Fiber 12.7g   45%
Total Sugars 10.6g
Protein 14.7g

Lunch

Tomato Soup

This soup calls for fewer ingredients but tastes great. It is a soup loved by kids as well as adults.

Cooking Time: 15 Minutes
Yield: 2 Servings

Ingredients

6 cups tomatoes, chopped and peeled
1 teaspoon of olive oil
1 onion, peeled
4 cups vegetable broth
Salt and black pepper
1 tablespoon maple syrup
2 teaspoons lemon juice
1/2 cup cream
½ cup of water

Directions

Boil the tomatoes in boiling water for 10 minutes.
Peel the tomatoes and transfer to the blender.
Blend to make pure.
Take a skillet and add olive oil and onions.

Cook for 3 minutes.

Pour the vegetable broth and add tomato puree and season it with salt and black pepper.

Simmer for a few minutes, and add maple syrup and lemon juice.

Add a bit of water.

Cook for 5 more minutes.

Then add half of the cream and cook 5 minutes.

Serve with the topping of remaining cream.

Nutrition Facts
Servings: 2
Amount per serving
Calories   282
% Daily Value*
Total Fat 9.6g 12%
Saturated Fat 3.4g   17%
Cholesterol 11mg   4%
Sodium 1578mg   69%
Total Carbohydrate 36.7g   13%
Dietary Fiber 7.7g   27%
Total Sugars 25.2g
Protein 15.6g

Dinner

Instant Pot Acorn Squash with Cranberries

It is a simple recipe made using instant pot. It is a perfect low calories recipe to enjoy as dinner.

Cooking Time: 15 Minutes
Yield: 4 Servings

Ingredients

4 acorn squashes, trimmed and seedless
6 tablespoons of olive oil
2 shallots, chopped
12 ounces of mushrooms, chopped
4 garlic cloves, minced
1 cup cranberries

Directions

Pour the water in the instant pot, and adjust the trivet or steamer basket on top.
Place the squash on top of the steamer basket.
Lock the lid of the instant pot.
Set a timer to 5 minutes at high pressure.
Once the timer beeps, release the steam naturally.

Take a medium pan and heat oil then add shallots, mushrooms, and garlic.

Season it with salt and black pepper.

Cook for a few minutes, then add cranberries and let it cook for 4 more minutes.

Open the instant pot, and pour the sauce ingredients on top.

Serve.

Nutrition Facts

Servings: 4

Amount per serving

Calories 336

% Daily Value*

Total Fat 21.6g 28%

Saturated Fat 3.1g 15%

Cholesterol 0mg 0%

Sodium 14mg 1%

Total Carbohydrate 37g 13%

Dietary Fiber 10.9g 39%

Total Sugars 2.5g

Protein 5.3g

Snack

Herb-Crusted Asparagus Spears

It is a very light and easy to make vegetable recipe that can be enjoyed as a snack. It can be prepared as an alternative to French fries.

Cooking Time: 20 Minutes
Yield: 2 Servings

Ingredients

10 asparagus, washed
2 teaspoons of flax seeds
1 teaspoon of hemp seeds
1 teaspoon of ginger paste
¼ teaspoon of garlic paste
Salt and black pepper
¼ cup whole wheat bread crumbs
1/4 cup whole-wheat breadcrumbs
1 teaspoon of lime juice

Directions

Preheat your oven to 350°F.
Remove the white bottom from the end of the asparagus by snapping it off.

Combine all the remaining ingredients in a bowl and toss the asparagus with the mixture.

Arrange asparagus on a baking sheet lined with parchment paper.

Bake it in ovens or 20 minutes.

Once crispy, remove for oven

Then serve and enjoy.

Nutrition Facts

Servings: 2

Amount per serving

Calories 112

% Daily Value*

Total Fat 2.8g 4%

Saturated Fat 0.3g 2%

Cholesterol 0mg 0%

Sodium 102mg 4%

Total Carbohydrate 19g 7%

Dietary Fiber 3.6g 13%

Total Sugars 2.8g

Protein 5g

Drink/Smoothie

Chocolate Protein and Strawberry Shake

It is a very easy 5-minute smoothie recipe that is full of nutrients essential for the brain and body.

Cooking Time: 0 Minutes
Yield: 4 Servings

Ingredients

2 cups unsweetened almond milk
1 cup of strawberries, organic
2 scoops chocolate protein powder
½ cup of organic raw almonds
1 tablespoon organic MACA powder
1 tablespoon organic hemp seeds

Directions

Dump all the ingredients in a blender.
Pulse it for few seconds.
Pour into serving glasses and enjoy

Nutrition Facts
Servings: 4
Amount per serving

Calories 144
% Daily Value*
Total Fat 9.1g 12%
Saturated Fat 0.9g 5%
Cholesterol 10mg 3%
Sodium 130mg 6%
Total Carbohydrate 8.2g 3%
Dietary Fiber 3.2g 11%
Total Sugars 3.1g
Protein 9.1g

Dessert

Cherry Soft-Serve Ice Cream

It is a scrumptious plant-based dessert that is made with fresh cherries and tastes delicious and refreshing because of the addition of banana and vegan chocolate chips. It is a true family-friendly recipe that can be enjoyed by kids as well as adults.

Cooking Time: 0 Minutes
Yield: 3 Servings

Ingredients

4 bananas, ripped
1-1/2 cups cherries, frozen and organic
1/4 teaspoon of pure vanilla extract
1/4 cup almond milk
4 tablespoons of vegan chocolate chips

Directions

Dump all the listed ingredients in a food processor.
Pulse it for a few seconds.
Pour the mixture into a serving bowl and refrigerate for a few minutes.
Soft served ice-cream is ready to be a devourer.

Nutrition Facts

Servings: 3

Amount per serving

Calories 242

% Daily Value*

Total Fat 6.6g 9%

Saturated Fat 5.1g 25%

Cholesterol 0mg 0%

Sodium 12mg 1%

Total Carbohydrate 47.3g 17%

Dietary Fiber 5g 18%

Total Sugars 23g

Protein 2.6g

Day 7
Breakfast

Whole-Wheat Berry Muffins

If you are tired of trying the same old style breakfast, then incorporate these muffins in breakfast.

Cooking Time: 22 Minutes
Yield: 4 Servings

Ingredients

½ cup almond milk
1.5 tablespoon ground flaxseeds
1 teaspoon apple cider vinegar
2.5 cups whole-wheat pastry flour
2 teaspoons baking powder
¼ teaspoon baking soda
1/4 teaspoon salt
1/3 cup applesauce, unsweetened
1/3 cup pure maple syrup
1-1/3 teaspoons pure vanilla extract
1-1/3 cup blueberries

Directions

Preheat the oven to 375 degrees F.
Line a muffin paper with silicon liner.
Take a measuring cup and mix almond milk, vinegar, and flaxseeds.
Mix it vigorously for a few seconds.
Now, in a separate medium bowl, mix baking soda, baking powder, salt, and flour.
Now, pour the milk mixture into the flour mixture.
Next, add applesauce, vanilla, and maple syrup.
Next, fold in the blueberries.
Fill the muffin cup with batter and bake it in the oven for 22 minutes.
Once muffins are baked, let it get cooled completely for 10 minutes.
Remove from the tray and serve.
Enjoy.

Nutrition Facts
Servings: 4
Amount per serving
Calories   410
% Daily Value*
Total Fat 2.1g 3%
Saturated Fat 0.2g   1%
Cholesterol 0mg   0%
Sodium 252mg   11%

Total Carbohydrate 87.8g 32%
Dietary Fiber 4g 14%
Total Sugars 22.4g
Protein 9g

Lunch

Chickpea Cauliflower Quiche

It is a perfect lunchtime treat that tastes delicious and filled with all the nutrients essential for the brain and body.

Cooking Time: 30 Minutes
Yield: 4 Servings

Ingredients

2 cups chickpea flour
2 tablespoons of flax meal
Salt and black pepper, to taste
1 teaspoon Italian seasoning or Herbs de Provence
½ teaspoon of baking powder
1 small head of cauliflower
1 cup of water
1 zucchini, sliced
1 red onion, sliced thinly
1 cup of fresh rosemary, chopped

Directions

Combine all the dry ingredients in a small bowl.

Now chop onions and zucchinis and process cauliflower in a blender.
Add these vegetables to the bowl and mix in water.
Stir in remaining ingredients.
Mix well to a thick consistency.
Now, take an 8-inch silicon cake tin.
Now spoon the mixture to the tin.
Bake in oven for 30 minutes, at 350 degrees F.
Once golden from the top, serve and enjoy.

Nutrition Facts
Servings: 4
Amount per serving
Calories 442
% Daily Value*
Total Fat 9.9g 13%
Saturated Fat 1.8g 9%
Cholesterol 1mg 0%
Sodium 45mg 2%
Total Carbohydrate 73.6g 27%
Dietary Fiber 25.4g 91%
Total Sugars 11.8g
Protein 21.6g

Dinner

Indian Peanut Noodles

It is a fusion of noodles, peanuts, and vegetables that is perfect for busty weekend dinners.
The chutney is sweet and a bit savoury.

Cooking Time: 20 Minutes
Yield: 4-6 Servings

Peanut Chutney Ingredients

2 cups of raw peanuts
1 teaspoon cumin powder
1 teaspoon red chilli powder
1/4 teaspoon salt

Other Ingredients

10 ounces soba noodles
4 tablespoons vegetable oil
1 cup broccoli florets, chopped into 1-inch pieces
1 cup red bell pepper, chopped into 1-inch pieces
1/4 cup thinly sliced scallions, divided
1/2 cup carrots, peeled and chopped
1 cup zucchinis, chopped
1 to 2 tablespoons light soy sauce, to taste

Salt, to taste

Directions

Roast the peanut for 6 minutes in the microwave and then let it cool
Now, to prepare the sauce, blend all the chutney ingredients in a blender.
Cook the noodles according to package instruction.
In a skillet heat oil and broccoli, and sauté for 5minutes
Then add other vegetables one by one.
Do not overcook to make vegetables mushy.
Now add the chutney and mix well
Then add salt and soy sauce.
Now add noodles and mix well.
Serve it once done.

Nutrition Facts
Servings: 4
Amount per serving
Calories   806
% Daily Value*
Total Fat 50.4g   65%
Saturated Fat 7.8g   39%
Cholesterol 0mg   0%
Sodium 1919mg   83%
Total Carbohydrate 75.1g   27%

Dietary Fiber 8.1g   29%
Total Sugars 8.4g
Protein 31.4g

Snack

Peanut Butter and Chocolate Bars

These snack time bars combine hit combination of peanut butter and chocolate , to make it a mouth-watering treat to enjoy.

Cooking Time: 4 Minutes
Yield: 6 Servings

Ingredients

½ cup of coconut oil
2 cups cocoa powder, unsweetened
1 cup of peanut butter, no added sugar
¼ cup stevia
Salt, pinch

Directions

Pour oil in the skillet and let it melt on low flame.
Add butter and let it melt.
Cook it for 30 seconds.
Then add all the remaining ingredients and let it get combined well.
Cook utile all the ingredients are well combined and melted.

Pour the mixture into the baking sheet lined with parchment paper.
Freeze it for 40 minutes.
once solid ,serve it by cutting into bar shapes.

Nutrition Facts
Servings: 6
Amount per serving
Calories 473
% Daily Value*
Total Fat 43.6g 56%
Saturated Fat 22.5g 113%
Cholesterol 0mg 0%
Sodium 230mg 10%
Total Carbohydrate 24.2g 9%
Dietary Fiber 11.1g 40%
Total Sugars 4.5g
Protein 15.9g

Drink/ Smoothie

Raspberry Creamy Smoothie

It is a very nutritious smoothie that gives the body energy to kick start the routine.

Cooking Time: 0 Minutes
Yield: 2 Servings

Ingredients

1 cup baby spinach, chopped
2 cups raspberries, fresh
1/2 Roma tomato
10 ounces of Water
8 medium strawberries
Few ice cubes, for chilling

Directions

Dump all the ingredients into a high-speed blender
Pulse it for 30 seconds
Once smooth, pour into glasses and enjoy

Nutrition Facts
Servings: 2
Amount per serving

Calories 93
% Daily Value*
Total Fat 1.1g 1%
Saturated Fat 0g 0%
Cholesterol 0mg 0%
Sodium 22mg 1%
Total Carbohydrate 21.2g 8%
Dietary Fiber 9.8g 35%
Total Sugars 9.1g
Protein 2.7g

Dessert

Pumpkin Oatmeal Muffins

These are moist, aromatic, and perfect muffins for the autumn morning. These are naturally sweetened and are organic and gluten-free teat to enjoy.

Cooking Time: 28 Minutes
Yield: 4 Servings

Ingredients

½ cup cooked pumpkin
3 ripe bananas, mashed
½ cup unsweetened applesauce
1 cup rolled oats
1 tablespoon ground flaxseed meal
1 teaspoon pumpkin pie spice
¼ teaspoon of cinnamon
1 teaspoon of baking powder
1 teaspoon pure vanilla extract

Directions

Preheat the oven to 375 degrees F.
Line a muffin tray with parchment paper.
Take a bowl and mix all the ingredients.

Divide this batter amongst the muffin cups.
Bake in the oven for 28 minutes.
Once, its golden brown from the top take out from the oven.
Serve and enjoy.

Nutrition Facts
Servings: 4
Amount per serving
Calories 201
% Daily Value*
Total Fat 2.7g 3%
Saturated Fat 0.4g 2%
Cholesterol 0mg 0%
Sodium 7mg 0%
Total Carbohydrate 42.4g 15%
Dietary Fiber 6.8g 24%
Total Sugars 15.3g
Protein 4.8g

Day 8

Breakfast

Mason jar Overnight Oats

This oat recipe is the gluten-free and plant-based recipe. The almond milk can be replaced with any other plant-based milk, like coconut milk, or hemp milk. The recipe is prepared before a day.

Cooking Time: 0 Minutes
Yield: 2 Servings

Ingredients

½ cup gluten-free oats
1-1/4 cup almond milk
1 teaspoon of chia seeds
2 tablespoons maple syrup
½ teaspoon cinnamon
Dash of vanilla bean powder or extract
1 cup strawberries, chopped

Direction

Place oats, chia seeds, cinnamon, maple syrup, vanilla powder, and strawberries in a mason jar.

Mix and seal the jar.
Refrigerate overnight.
Next morning open the jar and mix the ingredients.
Serve and enjoy.

Nutrition Facts
Servings: 2
Amount per serving
Calories 971
% Daily Value*
Total Fat 37.9g 49%
Saturated Fat 25.7g 128%
Cholesterol 175mg 58%
Sodium 210mg 9%
Total Carbohydrate 41.6g 15%
Dietary Fiber 7.4g 26%
Total Sugars 26.5g
Protein 117.2g
Vitamin D 0mcg

Lunch

Cold Raw Peanut Soup

It is a delicious, healthy, and cold version of peanut soup that is made without the hustle of cooking.

Cooking Time: 0 Minutes
Yield: 2 Servings

Ingredients

½ cup of raw peanuts
4 cups of water
1 cup broccoli, fresh or frozen
½ cup spinach, fresh or frozen
½ cup of leeks, sliced
½ garlic clove, chopped
½ teaspoon ginger, grated
1 tablespoon of lemon juice
Salt and black pepper, to taste

Directions

Dump all the ingredients in a high-speed blender and pulse until smooth.
Once a smooth consistency is obtained serve it cold

It is a great-tasting and versatile soup to enjoy.

Nutrition Facts
Servings: 2
Amount per serving
Calories   250
% Daily Value*
Total Fat 18.3g   23%
Saturated Fat 2.6g   13%
Cholesterol 0mg   0%
Sodium 70mg 3%
Total Carbohydrate 13.5g   5%
Dietary Fiber 5.7g   20%
Total Sugars 3.2g
Protein 11.8g

Dinner

Zucchini with Stuffing

It is a perfect dish for weekend nights.

Cooking Time: 35 Minutes
Yield: 3 Servings

Ingredients

1-1/2 cup quinoa, rinsed
6 medium zucchini
1 cup cannellini beans, drained
2 large onions, chopped
½ cup black olives
½ cup almonds, chopped
4 cloves of garlic, chopped
2 tablespoons olive oil
1 cup of water
1 cup cream

Directions

Take an air fryer and preheat it at 375 degrees F for 5 minutes.
In a skillet, heat the oil and sauté onions and garlic. Cook onions for 2 minutes.

Add quinoa and water.
Let it cook for 5 minutes.
Afterwards add cannellini beans, black olives, and almonds.
Cook for 10 minutes.
Wash and cut the zucchini lengthwise and takeout the seeds.
Fill the cavity of zucchinis with skillet mixture.
Place it in air fryer and cook for 15 minutes
Afterward take out zucchini and top it with cream.
Serve and enjoy.

Nutrition Facts
Servings: 3
Amount per serving
Calories   770
% Daily Value*
Total Fat 28.9g   37%
Saturated Fat 5.6g   28%
Cholesterol 15mg   5%
Sodium 285mg   12%
Total Carbohydrate 104.3g   38%
Dietary Fiber 28.5g   102%
Total Sugars 14.7g
Protein 32.7g

Snack

Carrot Cake Oatmeal

It is a very filling breakfast recipe, which keeps your craving on the bay for a long time.

Cooking Time: 25 Minutes
Yield: 4 Servings

Main Ingredients

2 cups almond milk
1 cup oats, whole grain
½ cup of water
1 cup shredded carrot
1/3 cup raisins
¼ teaspoon vanilla extract
¼ teaspoon of cinnamon
¼ teaspoon of allspice
Salt, dash

Topping Ingredients

4 tablespoons of maple syrup
1/3 cup chopped walnuts
4 tablespoons of coconut, shredded

Directions

In a medium cooking pot, pour milk and add oats along with water.
Then cook for 10 minutes.
Once started to simmer, add carrots, vanilla extract, cinnamon, raisins, allspice, and salt.
Simmer for 10 more minutes.
Pour this mixture to the bowl and drizzle maples syrup on top
Add walnuts and coconut on top.
Serve and enjoy.

Nutrition Facts
Servings: 4
Amount per serving
Calories   537
% Daily Value*
Total Fat 37.9g   49%
Saturated Fat 27.5g   137%
Cholesterol 0mg   0%
Sodium 82mg 4%
Total Carbohydrate 48.2g   18%
Dietary Fiber 7.1g   25%
Total Sugars 25.1g   7g

Drink/Smoothie

Fruity Smoothie

The addition of mangoes makes it one of the heartiest drinks to enjoy.

Cooking Time: 0 Minutes
Yield: 4 Servings

Ingredients

2 large mangos, peeled and diced
4 cups peach, fresh
1/2 cup pumpkin seeds
¼ cup almond butter
1.5 cup of almond milk
Ice cubes, for chilling

Directions

Dump all the ingredients in a blender and pulse.
Once smooth consistency is obtained, pour into ice-filled servings glasses
Serve chilled.

Nutrition Facts
Servings: 4

Amount per serving
Calories 485
% Daily Value*
Total Fat 32.7g 42%
Saturated Fat 20.9g 104%
Cholesterol 0mg 0%
Sodium 19mg 1%
Total Carbohydrate 48g 17%
Dietary Fiber 8g 29%
Total Sugars 40.3g
Protein 9.9g

Dessert

Easy Brownies

It is a rich, plant-based, and incredibly delicious recipe that is made with easy ingredients
It is a satisfying gluten-free treat to enjoy.

Cooking Time: 20 Minutes
Yield: 8 Servings

Ingredients

3 cups of dates, pitted, soft and fresh
1 cup of warm water
1 cup peanut butter
6 tablespoons of coconut oil
1 cup of cocoa powder
1 cup raw walnuts, roughly chopped

Directions

Preheat oven at 375 degrees F.
Line a loaf pan with parchment paper.
Now, in a food processor blend dates.
Take out the dates into a bowl using a spoon.
Add hot water to blender and blender until a paste is formed.

Add peanut butter, walnuts, coconut oil, and cacao powder to the blender and pulse for few more minutes.
Layer a parchment paper on top.
Bake it in the oven for 15 minutes.
Then remove for the oven and carefully lift out using edges of parchment paper.
Let it cool for 20 minutes.
Enjoy warm or cooled.

Nutrition Facts
Servings: 8
Amount per serving
Calories   586
% Daily Value*
Total Fat 37.3g   48%
Saturated Fat 13.6g   68%
Cholesterol 0mg   0%
Sodium 153mg   7%
Total Carbohydrate 63.9g   23%
Dietary Fiber 11.5g   41%
Total Sugars 45.7g
Protein 15.4g

Day 9

Breakfast

Oats Pancakes

These flourless pancakes are easy to prepare with just four simple and healthy ingredients.

Cooking Time: 15 Minutes
Yield: 3 Servings

Ingredients

4 ripe bananas, peeled
2.5 cups rolled oats
1.5 cup almond milk
1 teaspoon of olive oil

Directions

Take a blender and add bananas, oats, and almond milk.
Once the batter is of smooth consistency, pour into a bowl.
Take a skillet, and heat oil in it over medium flame.
Now pour ½ cup of batter to the skillet and cook the pancakes.

Once bubbles formed on top, flip to cook from another side.

Once all batter is consumed, and pancake cakes are ready, serve.

Enjoy.

Nutrition Facts
Servings: 3
Amount per serving
Calories   688
% Daily Value*
Total Fat 35.1g   45%
Saturated Fat 26.5g   133%
Cholesterol 0mg   0%
Sodium 24mg 1%
Total Carbohydrate 88.7g   32%
Dietary Fiber 13.6g   49%
Total Sugars 23.9g
Protein 13.4g

Lunch

Avocado Toast

If you love avocadoes then this recipe is just for you. it is a slight savoury adn spicy .the texture is creamy and crunchy.

Cooking Time: 0 Minutes
Yield: 2 Servings

Ingredients

4 slices of bread
2 avocados, slices
Juice of 1 lemon
4 tablespoons pumpkin seeds
¼ teaspoon of red pepper flakes
1/3 teaspoon of smoked paprika
¼ teaspoon of sesame seeds
Salt and black pepper, to taste

Directions

First step is to toast the bread.
Now layer the avocado slices on the toast.
Squeeze lemon juice on top.

End with the sprinkle of pumpkin seeds, sesame seeds, pepper flakes, salt and black pepper .
Serve and enjoy.
Nutrition Facts
Servings: 2
Amount per serving
Calories 462
% Daily Value*
Total Fat 40.1g 51%
Saturated Fat 8.4g 42%
Cholesterol 0mg 0%
Sodium 135mg 6%
Total Carbohydrate 26.9g 10%
Dietary Fiber 14.1g 51%
Total Sugars 1.9g
Protein 5.4g

Dinner

Tofu and Peanut Satay

The fresh combination of tofu, mint, peanut, and coconut make this dish a classic. It is well paired with cucumber, which gives it a refreshing taste. It is a salty, tangy, and zesty recipe to enjoy at dinner time.

Cooking Time: 0 Minutes
Yield: 2 Servings

Ingredients

1 block of firm tofu, cubed
1 cucumber, ribbon

Ingredients for Marinade

1 tablespoon of peanut butter
4 tablespoons of tamari sauce
1 tablespoons of sesame oil
4 tablespoons of maple syrup
2 garlic cloves

Ingredients for Satay Sauce

1/3 cup coconut milk

4 tablespoons of peanut butter
2 tablespoons of peanut butter
2 teaspoons of lime juice
2 teaspoons tamari sauce
4 teaspoons of maple syrup
2 small garlic clove, minced
2 teaspoons of ginger, minced
Salt and black pepper, to taste

Directions

First, make a marinade in a bowl by mixing all the marinade ingredients.
Now, let the tofu sit in the marinade for 15 minutes.
Wash and peel the cucumber in thin ribbons.
Now, stir in the Satay ingredients together.
Thread the marinated tofu onto skewers.
Place the skewer on the grill and grill on medium flame.
Lightly oil it with oil spray.
Grill the tofu until lightly browned.
Now threat the cucumber on a skewer by folding it back forth to it easy thread to the skewer.
Top it with Satay drizzle and serve.

Nutrition Facts
Servings: 2
Amount per serving

Calories 787
% Daily Value*
Total Fat 46.6g 60%
Saturated Fat 14.6g 73%
Cholesterol 0mg 0%
Sodium 2528mg 110%
Total Carbohydrate 82.2g 30%
Dietary Fiber 7.1g 25%
Total Sugars 58g
Protein 23.5g

Snack

No Bake Oatmeal Bars

It is an excellent and healthy snack recipe that is chewy and sweet enough to satisfy sweet tooth.

Cooking Time: 0 Minutes
Yield: 3 Servings

Ingredients

1 cup   dates, soft and pitted
1/2 cup almonds
1/3 cup peanut butter, organic and all natural
2 tablespoons of maple syrup
3/4 cup oats
1/3 cup hemp seeds

Directions

Take a food processor ad place dates and almonds. Blend to mix well.
 Then add oats, peanut butter, hemp seeds, maple syrup and pulse for few minutes
Line a loaf pan with a parchment paper and press then prepares dough into the pan.
Freeze until solid and then cut in to equal squares.

Serve and enjoy.

Nutrition Facts
Servings: 3
Amount per serving
Calories 614
% Daily Value*
Total Fat 30g 38%
Saturated Fat 4.3g 21%
Cholesterol 0mg 0%
Sodium 136mg 6%
Total Carbohydrate 77.2g 28%
Dietary Fiber 10.9g 39%
Total Sugars 49.1g
Protein 19.1g

Drink/Smoothie

Snack Time Smoothie

The addition of almond milk makes it a nutritious smoothie to enjoy.

Cooking Time: 0 Minutes
Yield: 2 Servings

Ingredients

1 cup Almond Milk, Unsweetened
2 tablespoons Cocoa Powder, unsweetened
6 pieces of almonds, powdered
½ scoop of stevia
½ cup crushed ice

Directions

Combine all the ingredients in a blender and pulse for a few seconds.
Pour into tall serving glasses and enjoy

Nutrition Facts
Servings: 2
Amount per serving
Calories 308

% Daily Value*
Total Fat 31.1g 40%
Saturated Fat 25.9g 130%
Cholesterol 0mg 0%
Sodium 19mg 1%
Total Carbohydrate 10.4g 4%
Dietary Fiber 4.7g 17%
Total Sugars 4.3g
Protein 4.5g

Dessert

Homemade Chocolate Ice-Cream

It is a perfect dessert time treat that is loved by kids.

Cooking Time: 0 Minutes
Yield: 6 Servings

Ingredients

3 cups raw cashew, pre-soaked and drained
3 cups almond milk, unsweetened
6 tablespoons cacao powder, organic
Salt, pinch
4 scoops of stevia

Directions

In a high-speed blender, pulse all the ingredients
Transfer this mixture to the plastic container.
Refrigerate for 6 hours.
Once solid, serve and enjoy.

Nutrition Facts
Servings: 6
Amount per serving
Calories   719

% Daily Value*
Total Fat 64.4g 83%
Saturated Fat 34.1g 171%
Cholesterol 0mg 0%
Sodium 56mg 2%
Total Carbohydrate 39g 14%
Dietary Fiber 10.7g 38%
Total Sugars 7.4g
Protein 17.2g

Day 10

Breakfast

Triple Berry Porridge

This porridge is prepared with the best quality ingredients, and it is a breakfast time hit.

Cooking Time: 10 Minutes
Yield: 2 Servings

Ingredients

½ cup Steel Cut Oats
1/4 cup Quinoa
1.5 cups water
1 cup organic blueberries, frozen
2 tablespoons of Maple syrup, optional
1 teaspoon of hemp seeds, optional

Directions

Take an instant pot and combine oats, quinoa, and water
Lock the lid and set the timer to 10 minutes at high.
Once timer beeps, release the steam naturally.

Stir the mixture and transfer to a serving bowl.
Mix blueberries, maple syrup, and hemp seeds.
Mix well and then serve.
Enjoy.

Nutrition Facts
Servings: 2
Amount per serving
Calories 291
% Daily Value*
Total Fat 6.3g 8%
Saturated Fat 0.6g 3%
Cholesterol 0mg 0%
Sodium 10mg 0%
Total Carbohydrate 51.9g 19%
Dietary Fiber 5.6g 20%
Total Sugars 19.3g
Protein 8.7g

Lunch

Tofu Tikka Masala in Instant Pot

It is a very versatile dish with the true flavors of curry.

Cooking Time: 35 Minutes
Yield: 4 Servings

Ingredients

Tofu Tikka Masala Ingredients

20 tablespoons thick coconut milk
1 teaspoon coriander powder
½ teaspoon Garam Masala
½ teaspoon red chili powder
½ teaspoon smoked paprika
Salt, to taste
400 grams extra-firm tofu

Curry Ingredients

4 tablespoons olive oil
3 red onion, chopped
3 garlic cloves, finely chopped
2-inches ginger, chopped

8 large tomatoes, pureed
1 teaspoon curry powder
½ teaspoon cumin powder
Salt, to taste
¼ teaspoon red chili powder
2 teaspoons honey
1 cup of coconut milk
1/2 cup water

Directions

Combine all the tofu Tikka Masala ingredients in a large bowl.
Mix well and set it aside.
Now make curry.
In a skillet heat oil and make curry by adding onions, ginger, garlic and tomatoes
Cook it for about 5 minutes.
Then add remaining ingredients from the curry ingredients.
Simmer it for 10 minutes.
Now, add tofu mixture from the bowl into the skillet.
Close the lid and cook for 20 minutes.
Once done, serve.

Nutrition Facts
Servings: 4
Amount per serving

Calories 641
% Daily Value*
Total Fat 53g 68%
Saturated Fat 31.2g 156%
Cholesterol 0mg 0%
Sodium 91mg 4%
Total Carbohydrate 36.2g 13%
Dietary Fiber 10g 36%
Total Sugars 21.1g
Protein 17.5g

Dinner

Simple Spinach Soup

It is a very healthy soup recipe that is rich in mineral, protein, and vitamins.

Cooking Time: 12 Minutes
Yield: 6 Servings

Ingredients

10 cups vegetable broth
1 cup tomatoes, un-drained
1 cup spinach, thawed and drained
Salt and black pepper, to taste
½ cup carrot
4 cloves garlic, minced
1 onion, peeled and chopped
1/3 cup celery
½ teaspoon chilli powder
¼ teaspoon curry powder
2 cups of coconut milk

Directions

Combine all ingredients in an Instant Pot.
Set timer for 12 minutes at high pressure.

After 12 minutes, let the pressure release naturally.

Turn on the sauté mode and add milk, cook for 2 minutes.

Serve in soup bowls.

Nutrition Facts

Servings: 6

Amount per serving

Calories   271

% Daily Value*

Total Fat 21.5g   28%

Saturated Fat 17.6g   88%

Cholesterol 0mg   0%

Sodium 1301mg   57%

Total Carbohydrate 11g   4%

Dietary Fiber 3.1g   11%

Total Sugars 6g

Protein 10.8g

Snack

Strawberries Popsicles

These popsicles are delicious and easy to make.

Cooking Time: 0 Minutes
Yield: 2 Servings

Ingredients

½ cups coconut milk
4 cups strawberries
2 scoops of stevia
1/3 cup water

Directions

Blend all the listed ingredients in a blender and pulse it into a smooth paste
Refrigerate for a few hours or overnight
Once, sold enjoy as a sweet snack time treat.

Nutrition Facts
Servings: 2
Amount per serving
Calories   230
% Daily Value*

Total Fat 15.2g 19%
Saturated Fat 12.7g 63%
Cholesterol 0mg 0%
Sodium 13mg 1%
Total Carbohydrate 25.5g 9%
Dietary Fiber 7.1g 25%
Total Sugars 16.1g
Protein 3.3g

Drink/Smoothie

Green Smoothie Recipe

It is a great-tasting and energy boasting, smoothie that can be enjoyed at any time of the day.
It is rich, creamy, and thick

Cooking Time: 0 Minutes
Yield: 2 Servings

Ingredients

2 bananas, ripped
1 cup spinach
2/3 cup almond milk
4 tablespoons of peanut butter

Directions

Pulse all the ingredients in a blender and make a smooth paste.
Pour into serving glasses.
Enjoy it chilled.

Nutrition Facts
Servings: 2
Amount per serving

Calories 480
% Daily Value*
Total Fat 35.6g 46%
Saturated Fat 20.5g 102%
Cholesterol 0mg 0%
Sodium 172mg 7%
Total Carbohydrate 38.2g 14%
Dietary Fiber 7.1g 25%
Total Sugars 20.2g
Protein 11.6g

Dessert

Dessert Time Parfait

It is a very easy recipe that combines coconut yogurt, bananas, and apple in one bowl.
You can also add a few other fruits of your own choice to make it tastier.

Cooking Time: 0 Minutes
Yield: 3 Servings

Ingredients

1 cup of coconut yogurt
1 cup berries
1 cup bananas, peeled and chopped
1 cup apples, chopped
1 cup Granola
1 cup almonds, chopped

Directions

Take a bowl, and layer granola, then yogurt followed by fruits, and almonds.
Repeat this step twice and then refrigerate for a few hours
Once it's done, serve

Nutrition Facts
Servings: 3
Amount per serving
Calories 426
% Daily Value*
Total Fat 37.2g 48%
Saturated Fat 5.6g 28%
Cholesterol 0mg 0%
Sodium 22mg 1%
Total Carbohydrate 82.5g 30%
Dietary Fiber 16.1g 58%
Total Sugars 39.5g
Protein 21.6g

Day 11

Breakfast

Keto Cinnamon Coffee

It is delicious and easy to make a recipe that energizes the body and provide full nutrition. The combination of cinnamon and coffee is classic.

Cooking Time: 0 Minutes
Yield: 2 Servings

Ingredients

4 teaspoons of grounded coffee
1 teaspoon of cinnamon
2 cups of water, hot

Directions

Take coffee brewer, and mix cinnamon powder and ground coffee.
Pour in piping hot water to the brewer.
Let it brew.
Then press it and pour it into the cup.
Serve.

Nutrition Facts
Servings: 2
Amount per serving
Calories 3
% Daily Value*
Total Fat 0g 0%
Saturated Fat 0g 0%
Cholesterol 0mg 0%
Sodium 8mg 0%
Total Carbohydrate 0.9g 0%
Dietary Fiber 0.6g 2%
Total Sugars 0g
Protein 0.1g

Lunch

Baked Veggies with Sauce

All the healthy ingredients are part of this recipe, and it is prepared the most simple way. It is a low-fat recipe to enjoy.

Cooking Time: 30 Minutes
Yield: 2 Servings

Main Ingredients

2 Cups Broccoli Raw, chopped
¼ Cup cauliflower florets
¼ cup cabbage
¼ cup kale
¼ small tomatoes, chopped

Sauce Ingredients

2 Ounces Chia Seeds
10 tablespoons Almond
1 lime, juiced
1 tablespoons Garlic
Salt and Black Pepper
4 tablespoons of olive oil

Directions

Pulse all the sauce ingredients in the blender to prepare a paste.

In a bowl, combine all the ingredients listed below the main ingredients.

Drizzle the blended sauce over the top.

Bake it on the oven for 375 degrees for about 30 minutes.

Once baked, take out from the oven and enjoy.

Nutrition Facts
Servings: 2
Amount per serving
Calories   601
% Daily Value*
Total Fat 52.2g   67%
Saturated Fat 5.1g   26%
Cholesterol 0mg   0%
Sodium 41mg 2%
Total Carbohydrate 30.3g   11%
Dietary Fiber 19g   68%
Total Sugars 3.7g
Protein 15.8g

Dinner

Coconut Cabbage Stew

It is a very creamy and healthy version of stew to enjoy with steam brown rice.

Cooking Time: 20 Minutes
Yield: 2 Servings

Ingredients

2 tablespoons of olive oil
1 red onion, peeled and chopped
Salt and black pepper, to taste
2 large cloves of garlic, diced
1 teaspoon red chili powder
½ tablespoon mustard seeds
½ tablespoon curry powder
½ tablespoon turmeric powder
3 cups cabbage, quartered and shredded
½ cup carrot, peeled and sliced
4 tablespoons lemon juice
2 cups unsweetened coconut milk
⅓ Cup water

Topping

1 cup almond and cream, topping
Side serving
2 servings of steamed brown rice

Directions

Take a skillet and heat olive oil in it.
Cook the onions, in it for 1 minute, and add garlic.
Once the aroma comes, add salt, mustard seeds, curry powder, turmeric powder, and red chili powder.
Mix well, and add all the remaining ingredients excluding, coconut milk, and topping.
Cook covered for 10 minutes.
Afterward pour coconut milk and simmer for a few minutes.
Once it's done, serve with the topping of cashew cream.
Serve it with your favorite plant-based side serving.
Nutrition Facts
Servings: 2
Amount per serving
Calories   260
% Daily Value*
Total Fat 17.4g   22%
Saturated Fat 2.4g   12%
Cholesterol 0mg   0%

Sodium 54mg 2%
Total Carbohydrate 25.8g   9%
Dietary Fiber 6.4g   23%
Total Sugars 8.1g
Protein 4.3g

Snack

Fat Bombs

It is a very easy, satisfying, and sweet treat to enjoy.

Cooking Time: 5 Minutes
Yield: 2 Servings

Ingredients

1-1/2 cups shredded coconut flakes
1/4 cup organic nut butter
Pinch of cinnamon
¼ teaspoon of vanilla extract

Directions

Take a skillet and heat it over a medium pan.
Roast the coconut flakes in the pan and then add nut butter, cinnamon, and vanilla extract.
Transfer the mixture to the bowl and mix all the ingredients with hand and make small candy sized balls.
Refrigerate for a few minutes.
Once it's solid, serve.

Nutrition Facts

Servings: 2

Amount per serving

Calories 222

% Daily Value*

Total Fat 20.3g 26%

Saturated Fat 12.4g 62%

Cholesterol 0mg 0%

Sodium 33mg 1%

Total Carbohydrate 7.1g 3%

Dietary Fiber 5.1g 18%

Total Sugars 3.1g

Protein 4.5g

Drink/Smoothie

Sunrise Smoothie

Everyone needs some sunshine in their lives, so here is the recipe to enjoy.

Cooking Time: 0 Minutes
Yield: 2 Servings

Ingredients

1 cup unsweetened almond milk
1 cup oranges, peeled and seedless
1 cup of pomegranate
2 medium bananas
1 cup unsweetened strawberries 182 grams
2 tablespoons chia seed

Directions

Dump all the ingredients in a blender and pulse for few minutes.
Once smooth inconsistency.
Pour into ice-filled serving glasses and enjoy.
Nutrition Facts
Servings: 2

Amount per serving
Calories 273
% Daily Value*
Total Fat 3.5g 4%
Saturated Fat 0.4g 2%
Cholesterol 0mg 0%
Sodium 94mg 4%
Total Carbohydrate 63.1g 23%
Dietary Fiber 9.8g 35%
Total Sugars 38.4g
Protein 4.2g

Dessert

Keto Vanilla Custard

It is a very declivous, thick, and yummy treat that uses unsweetened almond milk. You can also replace almond milk with coconut milk, or any other plant-based milk.

Cooking Time: 15 Minutes
Yield: 2 Servings

Ingredients

6 egg yolks
1 cup unsweetened almond milk
½ teaspoon vanilla extract
2 tablespoons of maple syrup
4 tablespoons coconut oil

Directions

In a bowl, whisk the eggs and add vanilla extract, milk, maple syrup.
Then slowly add coconut oil.
Take a large pan and boil water in it.
Place the mixing bowl over simmering water.

Cook it until internal temperate reaches 140 degrees F.

Take out the bowl and then serve and enjoy.

Nutrition Facts

Servings: 2

Amount per serving

Calories   471

% Daily Value*

Total Fat 42.5g   55%

Saturated Fat 28.6g   143%

Cholesterol 629mg   210%

Sodium 116mg   5%

Total Carbohydrate 16.4g   6%

Dietary Fiber 0.5g   2%

Total Sugars 12.3g

Protein 8.6g

Day 12

Breakfast

Savoury Cauliflower Bread

It is perfect savoury bread that is versatile and different then regular bread.

Cooking Time: 20-22 Minutes
Yield: 2-3 Servings

Ingredients

2 cups almond flour
2 eggs, whisked
4 tablespoons of flaxseed
1 cup of cauliflower florets, grated
1 cup of buttermilk
4 tablespoons of butter, melted
Pinch of salt

Directions

Use a food processor to grate the cauliflower.
Then add almond flour, flax seed.

Then add liquid ingredients including butter, and buttermilk.

Whisk egg in a bowl and add it to the blender.

Add pinch of salt and pulse the ingredients.

Oil greased loaf pan and pour the mixture in it.

Pour 1 cup water in instant pot and adjust trivet on top.

Make a sling of the aluminium foil and place it on trivet

Put the loaf pan on top of the trivet.

Lock the lid of the instant pot and cook for 20 minutes, at high pressure.

Once the timer beeps, release the steam naturally.

Let it put it on a cooling rack.

Once cool serve.

Enjoy.

Nutrition Facts
Servings: 3
Amount per serving
Calories   380
% Daily Value*
Total Fat 30.8g   40%
Saturated Fat 12.2g   61%
Cholesterol 153mg   51%
Sodium 306mg   13%
Total Carbohydrate 12.6g   5%
Dietary Fiber 5.4g   19%

Total Sugars 5.1g
Protein 12.9g

Lunch

Pasta Salad

This filling veggie-packed lunch, is full of great taste and nutrition. The basil is added for extra flavor and aroma.

Cooking Time: 35 Minutes
Yield: 4 Servings

Ingredients

10 ounces penne pasta
8-ounces of green beans
1 tablespoon of olive oil
1 cup jalapeno, chopped
1 tablespoon of minced garlic
2 cherry tomatoes
½ cup dry white wine vinegar
Salt and black pepper, to taste
2 tablespoons of fresh thyme

Directions

Cook pasta according to package instruction.

When only 5 minutes remain, add green beans and reserve 1 cup of water from the pasta, for further use.
Drain pasta and green beans.
Take a skillet and add oil in it.
Cook it for 5 minutes.
Next, add garlic to the skillet and add tomatoes.
Cook until juice comes out.
Now, pour wine and cook until it evaporates.
Add pasta, green beans, and jalapenos.
Pour in the reserved water.
Add seasoning and thyme.
Cook for 10 minutes, or until the liquid evaporated.
Then serve and enjoy.

Nutrition Facts
Servings: 4
Amount per serving
Calories   283
% Daily Value*
Total Fat 5.6g 7%
Saturated Fat 0.8g   4%
Cholesterol 52mg   17%
Sodium 28mg 1%
Total Carbohydrate 48.4g   18%
Dietary Fiber 3.9g   14%
Total Sugars 3.4g
Protein 10.1g

Dinner

Zucchini-Mushroom Bowl

It is a satisfying dinner time bowl that is packed with nutritional and healthy ingredients.

Cooking Time: 20 Minutes
Yield: 4 Servings

Ingredients

2 medium zucchinis
Salt and black pepper, as needed
3 tablespoons of olive oil
1 cup onion
4 garlic cloves, minced
1 cup cremini mushrooms, chopped
1 tablespoon of tomato paste
1 cup tomatoes, chopped and fried
6 ounces fresh baby spinach, chopped
½ cup fresh basil, chopped

Directions

Take a vegetable peeler and peel the zucchini.
Toss the salt and black pepper to the zucchini.

Take a Dutch oven and heat oil in it over medium flame.
Add garlic and onion and cook for 5 minutes.
Next, add mushroom and cook for 5 minutes.
Add tomato paste, tomatoes, pepper and salt.
Reduce the heat to medium and simmer occasionally.
Then add in striped zucchinis and baby spinach.
Sprinkle basil at the end.
Serve and enjoy.

Nutrition Facts
Servings: 4
Amount per serving
Calories   148
% Daily Value*
Total Fat 11.1g   14%
Saturated Fat 1.6g   8%
Cholesterol 0mg   0%
Sodium 52mg 2%
Total Carbohydrate 11.9g   4%
Dietary Fiber 3.6g   13%
Total Sugars 5.1g
Protein 4g

Snack

Herbed Potato Hummus

It is very easy to prepare hummus that combines some aromatic herbs, and its best served with baked potatoes.

Cooking Time: 0 Minutes
Yield: 24 Servings

Ingredients

1 cup of basil leaves
3 cups of garbanzo beans
1 cup vegetable broth
½ cup parsley leaves, lightly packed
¼ cup lemon juice, squeezed
4 tablespoons sesame seeds, toasted
3 cloves garlic
1 cup chopped chives
2 baked potatoes

Directions

Chop all the listed ingredients in a blender, excluding baked potatoes.

Once the smooth consistency is achieved, serve it with a baked potato.

Nutrition Facts

Servings: 4

Amount per serving

Calories   686

% Daily Value*

Total Fat 14.3g   18%

Saturated Fat 1.9g   9%

Cholesterol 0mg   0%

Sodium 245mg   11%

Total Carbohydrate 110.7g   40%

Dietary Fiber 29.1g   104%

Total Sugars 17.5g

Protein 34.6g

Drink/Smoothie

3 Berries Smoothie

It is a pretty simple and delicious recipe to enjoy.

Cooking Time: 0 Minutes
Yield: 2 Servings

Ingredients

1 cup raspberries
½ cup strawberries
½ cup blueberries
1 cup almond milk
½ inch ginger cube
Pinch of salt
Pinch of black pepper

Directions

Pulse all the ingredients in a blender until a smooth consistency is formed.
Pour into ice-filled serving glasses and enjoy.

Nutrition Facts
Servings: 2
Amount per serving
Calories   340

% Daily Value*
Total Fat 29.3g 38%
Saturated Fat 25.4g 127%
Cholesterol 0mg 0%
Sodium 97mg 4%
Total Carbohydrate 22g 8%
Dietary Fiber 8.3g 29%
Total Sugars 12.1g
Protein 4g

Dessert

Keto Vanilla Pannacotta

It is naturally sweetened dessert, which is purely healthy and creamy.

Cooking Time: 10 Minutes
Yield: 2 Servings

Ingredients

1 teaspoon gelatin powder
1 cup of water, for mixing
2 cups heavy whipping cream
1 tablespoon vanilla extract
1 pomegranate, seeds

Directions

Pour water in a bowl, and soak the gelatin powder in it.
Let it sit for 5 minutes.
Next, take a pan, and add vanilla extract and cream in it.
Simmer the mixture for a few minutes.
Once the cream gets thick, add gelatin.
Mix well and then turn off the flame.

Pour the cream into serving bowls.
Refrigerate it for a few hours.
Once it's solid, serve with the topping of pomegranate seeds.
Enjoy.

Nutrition Facts
Servings: 2
Amount per serving
Calories 494
% Daily Value*
Total Fat 44.4g 57%
Saturated Fat 27.6g 138%
Cholesterol 164mg 55%
Sodium 57mg 2%
Total Carbohydrate 17.2g 6%
Dietary Fiber 0.5g 2%
Total Sugars 11.5g
Protein 6g

Day 13

Breakfast

Raspberry Truffle Brownies

These are yummy, mouth-watering, and fudgy brownie recipe, which is very stiff. The raspberries add extra flour to the brownie.

Cooking Time: 15 Minutes
Yield: 4 Servings

Ingredients

6 ounces unsweetened chocolate, chopped
1/3 cup raspberry jam
½ cup of cane sugar
1/3 cup unsweetened applesauce
1 teaspoon pure vanilla extract
¼ teaspoon almond extract
1.5 cups whole wheat pastry flour
½ cup unsweetened cocoa powder
¼ teaspoon baking powder
½ teaspoon baking soda
¼ teaspoon salt
1-1/2 cup raspberries, frozen or fresh

Directions

Preheat the oven to 375 degrees F.
Line a parchment paper baking dish.
Take a bowl and melt chocolate in it.
Take a bowl and mix all the dry ingredients.
In another bowl, add all the wet ingredients.
Mix all the ingredients well.
Fold and mix the ingredients of both the bowl.
Spread this mixture into the prepared pan.
Bake the brownies in preheated oven for 15 minutes.
Once done, take out to let it get cool.
Serve.
 Nutrition Facts
Servings: 4
Amount per serving
Calories   335
% Daily Value*
Total Fat 23.9g   31%
Saturated Fat 14.6g   73%
Cholesterol 0mg   0%
Sodium 185mg   8%
Total Carbohydrate 42.7g   16%
Dietary Fiber 12.9g   46%
Total Sugars 16.6g
Protein 8.1g

Lunch

Broccoli Lemon Pasta

A very easy and low-calorie pasta recipe that is yummy and delicious and made with whole-grain pasta for more health and flavor.

Cooking Time: 35-40minutes
Yield: 3 servings

Ingredients

1 pound of broccoli, crowns
1/3 cup of vegetable oil
1 lemon, sliced
6 ounces of whole grained shell pasta
2 tablespoons of butter
2 garlic cloves, minced
1/4 teaspoon red pepper
3/4 teaspoon salt
1/2 teaspoon black pepper
2 teaspoons lemon zest

Directions

Preheat the oven to 450degrees F.

Toss chopped broccoli with oil.
Layer broccoli in a baking dish.
Arrange lemon in the side.
Bake it in the oven for 15 minutes until tender.
In a Dutch oven bring the water to the boil.
Cook the pasta according to package instruction in a Dutch oven.
Drain and reserve the pasta liquid.
Now remove the pasta from Dutch oven and dry the Dutch oven with paper towel.
Heat it at medium flame and then cook the butter until browned.
Melt butter in a Dutch oven over medium-high.
Cook until browned and very fragrant, about 3 minutes.
Add the garlic and red peppers.
Stir generously.
Then add in pasta and season it with salt and black pepper.
Add reserved liquid and broccoli.
Cook for 10 more minutes until liquid evaporates.
Top with lemon zest and enjoy.

Nutrition Facts
Servings: 3
Amount per serving
Calories   504
% Daily Value*

Total Fat 33.7g 43%
Saturated Fat 9.8g 49%
Cholesterol 62mg 21%
Sodium 701mg 30%
Total Carbohydrate 42.7g 16%
Dietary Fiber 4.2g 15%
Total Sugars 3.1g
Protein 11g

Dinnerr

Sweet Potato Soup

This easy and flavorful sweet potato soup is warming and delicious with addition of buttery avocado and crispy tortilla strips or chips on top.

Cooking Time: 65 Minutes
Yield: 3 Servings

Ingredients

1 large sweet potato
2 cups of vegetable broth
½ cup of almond milk
2 garlic cloves
1 teaspoon of chipotle powder
1 teaspoon of lime juice

Topping

1 avocado, pitted
1 cup corn chips
Dash of smoky paprika
1 tablespoon of lime juice

Directions

Preheat the oven to 430 degrees F.
Pierce in sweet potatoes and bake in oven for 55 minutes.
Peel off the skin of potatoes and set aside for further use.
In a blender, pulse together milk, broth, potato flesh, garlic, lime, and chipotle powder.
Adjust the seasoning by adding salt and black pepper.
Now pour the soup into a cooking pot add simmer at low heat.
Once hot serve into serving bowls.
Top with all the toppings.
Serve hot.

Nutrition Facts
Servings: 3
Amount per serving
Calories 673
% Daily Value*
Total Fat 41.8g 54%
Saturated Fat 13.3g 66%
Cholesterol 0mg 0%
Sodium 2801mg 122%
Total Carbohydrate 70g 25%
Dietary Fiber 14.5g 52%

Total Sugars 14.5g
Protein 7.5g

Snack

Raw Broccoli Poppers

Best popper that are pure plant based and vegan.

Cooking Time: 7 Hours (Dehydrate)
Yield: 2 Servings

Ingredients

2 cups broccoli florets, washed and chopped
½ cup cashews, soaked overnight
½ red bell pepper, chopped and seeds removed
2 tablespoons lemon juice, squeezed
1/6 cup water
2 teaspoons of nutritional yeast
1/2 teaspoon of onion powder
½ teaspoon of turmeric powder
Salt and black pepper, to taste

Directions

Take a high-speed blender and pulse cashews in it.
Take a container and chop red bell peppers in it.
Then add lemon juice, nutritional yeast, water, onion powder, salt, and turmeric powder

Process it for 45 seconds.
Take a bowl and place broccoli in it.
Add container mixture and then cashew cream.
Mix it and coat broccoli well with the mixture.
Dehydrate at 125 degrees F for 7 hours.
Once, its crunchy take out the broccoli.
Serve and enjoy.

Nutrition Facts
Servings: 2
Amount per serving
Calories   257
% Daily Value*
Total Fat 16.6g   21%
Saturated Fat 3.3g   17%
Cholesterol 0mg   0%
Sodium 42mg 2%
Total Carbohydrate 22.2g   8%
Dietary Fiber 4.9g   17%
Total Sugars 5.3g
Protein 9.9g

Drink/Smoothie

Classic Smoothed Recipe

As by the name, it is a classic recipe that combines some finest fruits and vegetables in one glass.

Cooking Time: 0 Minutes
Yield: 4 Servings

Ingredients

2 cups of apples
2 cups of almond milk
¼ cup flax seeds
¼ cup protein powder, soy protein
1 cup spinach
½ cup kale
2 bananas, peeled

Directions

Pulse all the ingredients in a blender and pour into ice-filled serving glasses.
Enjoy.

Nutrition Facts

Servings: 4

Amount per serving

Calories   489

% Daily Value*

Total Fat 32.2g   41%

Saturated Fat 26.2g   131%

Cholesterol 32mg   11%

Sodium 59mg 3%

Total Carbohydrate 40.5g   15%

Dietary Fiber 9.1g   32%

Total Sugars 23.4g

Protein 16.5g

Dessert

Chia Seed Pudding

The super ingredients know as chia seed is a part of this pudding that is a very healthy alternative to any high calories pudding.

Cook Time: 0 Minutes
Yield: 2 Serving

Ingredients

½ cup of brewed coffee (chilled)
1 cup of coconut milk
2 tablespoons almond butter
½ teaspoon of vanilla extract
4 tablespoons of maple syrup
2 tablespoons of unsweetened cocoa powder
1/3 cup of chia seeds

Directions

The first step is to brew the coffee.
Afterward, blend coffee with coconut milk.
Then add maple syrup, vanilla extract, and cacao powder .

Mix it very well .
Next, add almond butter.
Pour the mixture to a jar and add Chia seeds.
Shake well and let it sit in the refrigerator for 3 hours.
Once chilled, serve.
Enjoy.
 Nutrition Facts
Servings: 2
Amount per serving
Calories   701
% Daily Value*
Total Fat 51.5g   66%
Saturated Fat 27.9g   140%
Cholesterol 0mg   0%
Sodium 32mg 1%
Total Carbohydrate 57.4g   21%
Dietary Fiber 20.6g   74%
Total Sugars 28.7g
Protein 14.3g

Day 14

Breakfast

Lemon Muffins

It is easy to prepare a breakfast recipe that includes some delicious ingredients like almond milk, chia seed, and coconut oil.

Cooking Time: 25 Minutes
Yield: 4 Servings

Ingredients

10 tablespoons of warm water
4 tablespoons of ground flaxseed
½ teaspoon vanilla extract
3 cups gluten-free flour, all-purpose
½ teaspoon baking soda
¼ pinch of salt
½ cup almond milk
1/3 cup maple syrup
1/4 cup coconut oil
2 teaspoons lemon zest, finely grated
½ tablespoon lemon juice
1/4 cup chia seeds

Directions

Preheat the oven to 375 degrees F.
Linea muffin tray with muffin cups.
Take a bowl, and mix water, flaxseed, and set it aside for soaking.
In a separate bowl, mix lemon juice, maple syrup, vanilla, oil, lemon zest, milk, and beat it until smooth.
Then add soaked flaxseeds, and use a spatula to mix it well.
Now, combine baking soda, flour, salt, and chia seeds.
Mix it into a smooth paste.
Pour the batter into muffin cups and sprinkle chia seeds on top.
Bake in the oven for 25 minutes.
Let it sit for 10 minutes before serving.
Enjoy.

Nutrition Facts
Servings: 4
Amount per serving
Calories   572
% Daily Value*
Total Fat 24.7g   32%
Saturated Fat 19g   95%
Cholesterol 0mg   0%

Sodium 406mg 18%
Total Carbohydrate 82.3g 30%
Dietary Fiber 11.5g 41%
Total Sugars 18.8g
Protein 6.8g

Lunch

Tofu Chow Mein

It is a very easy and yummy treat that is prepared with tofu, pasta, and a hint of sesame oil that gives it a great taste and flavor.

Cooking Time: -20 Minutes
Yield: 4 Servings

Ingredients

10 ounces whole-wheat angel hair pasta, uncooked
4 tablespoons sesame oil, divided
20 ounces of extra-firm tofu
1-1/2 cups sliced fresh mushrooms
2 sweet red peppers, julienned
1/2 cup reduced-sodium soy sauce
4 green onions, thinly sliced

Directions

Take a large cooking pot and cook the pasta in boiling water, according to package instructions.
In a skillet, heat the oil and cook onions for 2 minutes.

Then add mushrooms, pepper, and tofu.

Then add cooked and drained pasta and stir fry mushrooms, pepper, and tofu.

Simmer it for 5 minutes.

In the end, add soy sauce and serve.

Nutrition Facts

Servings: 4

Amount per serving

Calories 766

% Daily Value*

Total Fat 24.6g 32%

Saturated Fat 2.7g 14%

Cholesterol 0mg 0%

Sodium 1104mg 48%

Total Carbohydrate 96.3g 35%

Dietary Fiber 17.1g 61%

Total Sugars 4.9g

Protein 39.5g

Dinner

Vegan Tacos

It is a very classic twist to a taco recipe as we are introducing all the ingredients that ate vegan and plant-based. It is one satisfying recipe to enjoy.

Cooking Time: 20 Minutes
Yield: 3 Servings

Ingredients

6 tortillas
1 cup refried beans
4 cups Portobello mushrooms, chopped
2 red bell peppers, chopped
1 onion, chopped

Chipotle Marinade

1 tablespoon sesame oil
2 tablespoons Chipotle in Adobo sauce
1 minced garlic clove, minced
¼ teaspoon cumin
¼ teaspoon coriander
Salt and black pepper, to taste

Toppings

½ cup pickled onions

1 avocado, pitted

Directions

Preheat the oven to 375 degrees F.

Slice the bell pepper and mushrooms in thick wedges.

Also, cut the onions in half-moons.

Place the ingredients in a sheet pan lined with a baking sheet.

Next, mix all the marinade ingredients in a bowl and brush the mushroom, red bell pepper, and onions with marinade.

Roast it for 20 minutes until tender.

Warm the tortilla and then spread refried beans on top.

Divide the oven mixture on top equally and then top it with fresh avocados and pickled onions.

Nutrition Facts

Servings: 3

Amount per serving

Calories   547

% Daily Value*

Total Fat 25.6g   33%

Saturated Fat 8g   40%

Cholesterol 20mg   7%

Sodium 1333mg 58%
Total Carbohydrate 70.5g 26%
Dietary Fiber 16.9g 60%
Total Sugars 10g
Protein 14.1g

Snack

Strawberry-Mango Ice

It is a mouth-watering shaved ice that is a perfect summer treat to enjoy.

Cooking Time: 10 Minutes
Yield: 4 Servings

Ingredients

3 cups sugar, divided
1-quart strawberries, diced
1 cup mango juice
1 Cup Toasted Coconut

Directions

Take a medium pot and bring water to boil about a cup.
Dissolve sugar in it.
Remove it from heat and add 2 cups of water.
Pour the mixture in a baking dish and freeze for 5 hours.
Stir it every 45 minutes.

Now, in a blender process the strawberries and remaining sugar.
Transfer it to container and pour mango juice in it .
Divide the ice into four serving glasses and divide the strawberry mixture and mango juice on top of each.
Enjoy.

Nutrition Facts
Servings: 4
Amount per serving
Calories   723
% Daily Value*
Total Fat 7.1g 9%
Saturated Fat 5.9g   30%
Cholesterol 0mg   0%
Sodium 9mg   0%
Total Carbohydrate 175.1g   64%
Dietary Fiber 4.9g   18%
Total Sugars 168.3g
Protein 1.7g

Drink/Smoothie

Chocolate Peanut Butter Shake

It is more than a smoothie and more of a dessert. It is one of the delicious, protein-based smoothie that is sweet, savory and creamy.

Cooking Time: 0 Minute
Yield: 4 Servings

Ingredients

4 bananas, peeled
2 tablespoons of cacao powder
4 tablespoons of peanut butter
1 cup of almond milk

Directions

Combine all the listed ingredients in a blender and pulse until smooth.
Pour into tall serving glasses and enjoy.
 Nutrition Facts
Servings: 4
Amount per serving
Calories   362

% Daily Value*
Total Fat 24.7g 32%
Saturated Fat 15.8g 79%
Cholesterol 0mg 0%
Sodium 84mg 4%
Total Carbohydrate 38.4g 14%
Dietary Fiber 8.3g 30%
Total Sugars 17.9g
Protein 8.7g

Dessert

Cinnamon Spiced Apples

It is a delicious dessert, best served over vegan vanilla ice-cream.

Cooking Time: 4 Hours
Yield: 4 Servings

Ingredients

1/3 cup sugar
1/4 cup packed brown sugar
1 tablespoon cornstarch
3 teaspoons ground cinnamon
1/8 teaspoon ground nutmeg
6 large Granny Smith apples, peeled and cut into eighths
1/4 cup butter, cubed
6 scoops of vegan ice-cream

Directions

Take a large mixing bowl, and mix the first five ingredients in it.
Place the mixture into a slow cooker.
Add apples to the cooker.

Top it with butter and cover the slow cooker. Cook for 4 hours until apples are tender. Serve with vegan ice-cream.

Nutrition Facts
Servings: 4
Amount per serving
Calories   520
% Daily Value*
Total Fat 24.2g   31%
Saturated Fat 11.8g   59%
Cholesterol 31mg   10%
Sodium 260mg   11%
Total Carbohydrate 79.5g   29%
Dietary Fiber 12.1g   43%
Total Sugars 61.8g
Protein 4.1g

Day 15

Breakfast

Vegetable Pancakes

These yummy vegetable pancakes fully serve you early morning by filing up the craving and hunger. If you are a big vegetable fan, then this recipe is just for you.

Cook Time: 10 -15 Minutes
Yield: 1-2 Servings

Ingredients

2 zucchinis, grated
1 yellow squash medium size, grated
2 carrots, grated
1 onion, chopped
1-1/2 cup of almond flour
4 tablespoons of arrowroot
2 teaspoons dried basil
2 teaspoons dried parsley
Salt and black pepper, to taste
3 tablespoons of coconut oil

¼ teaspoon baking powder

Directions

First, wash, peel, and grate all the vegetables.
Place them in a bowl and add almond flour, arrowroot powder, basil, parsley, salt, black pepper, and baking soda.
Add water and make a paste.
Heat coconut oil in a skillet and add the paste in form of pancakes.
Once brown from the bottom flip to cook form another side.
Once done, serve and enjoy.

Nutrition Facts
Servings: 2
Amount per serving
Calories   407
% Daily Value*
Total Fat 34.5g   44%
Saturated Fat 18.7g   94%
Cholesterol 0mg   0%
Sodium 72mg 3%
Total Carbohydrate 21g   8%
Dietary Fiber 6.9g   25%
Total Sugars 6.9g
Protein 9.6g

Lunch

Lunchtime Rice

This recipe is prepared with cauliflower and brown rice. The mint and lemon give it refreshing taste and aroma.

Cook Time: 25 Minutes
Yield: 2-3 Servings

Ingredients

1 cup onions, chopped
1 teaspoon of red chili peppers
1/4 teaspoon of turmeric
1 cup cauliflower florets, chopped
1 tomato, chopped
¼ cup virgin olive oil
Salt and black pepper, to taste
1 cup cooked brown rice

Directions

Heat oil in a large skillet and add onions and cook for 5 minutes.
Once slightly brown add tomatoes, chili powder, turmeric powder, salt, and black pepper.

Cook for 2 minutes.
Then add cauliflower florets.
Add 1/4 cup of water.
Cook until cauliflower gets tender.
Serve over cooked brown rice.
Once done, serve and enjoy.

Nutrition Facts

Servings: 2

Amount per serving

Calories 603

% Daily Value*

Total Fat 28g 36%

Saturated Fat 4.1g 21%

Cholesterol 0mg 0%

Sodium 23mg 1%

Total Carbohydrate 82.1g 30%

Dietary Fiber 6.3g 22%

Total Sugars 4.6g

Protein 9.1g

Dinner

Noodle-Free Pad Thai

very amazingly delicious recipe that is spicy and savory at the same time. It is a twist to the noodle pad Thai.

Cooking Time: 10-15 Minute
Yields: 4 Servings

Ingredients

1 cup tofu, extra firm
2 tablespoons of coconut amino
1 teaspoon of garlic sauce
1/6 teaspoon of turmeric
4 tablespoons of lime juice
1 teaspoon of red pepper flake
1 1/2 tablespoon of maple syrup

Vegetables

1 teaspoon of sesame oil
1 Serrano pepper
¼ cup of green onions, sliced
1 cups red cabbage, thinly sliced

1 red bell pepper
2 Tbsp tamari
4-5 large carrots
6 leaves of collard greens

For Serving Optional

1 cup of fresh cilantro
1 cup Crushed peanuts/peanut sauce
2 lime wedges

Directions

Take a small bowl and mix coconut amino, turmeric, lime juice, red pepper flakes, maple syrup, and chili garlic sauce.

Put it aside.

Heat a skillet over medium flame and add sesame oil to it.

Add onions, pepper, bell pepper, cabbage, and tamari.

Cook for 4 minutes.

Then add collard and carrots.

Add tofu to the skillet and cook for 5 minutes.

Divide the mixture between the serving plate and then serve with peanut sauce, cilantro, and lime wedges.

Nutrition Facts
Servings: 4
Amount per serving
Calories 757
% Daily Value*
Total Fat 57.5g 74%
Saturated Fat 10.5g 52%
Cholesterol 0mg 0%
Sodium 893mg 39%
Total Carbohydrate 39.3g 14%
Dietary Fiber 11.3g 40%
Total Sugars 18.3g
Protein 34.8g

Snack

Walnut Squash

In this recipe, coconut oil enhances the overall flavor of the dish.

Cooking Time: 15 Minutes
Yield:3 Servings

Ingredients

2 tablespoons of coconut oil
2 yellow squash, shredded
2 tomatoes, chopped
½ cup walnuts, chopped
2 cloves garlic, minced

Directions

Take a large pan and heat oil in it.
Add tomatoes and garlic.
Cook for 5 minutes and then add walnuts and squash.
Stir for 10 minutes.
Once done, serve.
 Nutrition Facts
Servings: 2
Amount per serving

Calories 368
% Daily Value*
Total Fat 32.7g 42%
Saturated Fat 12.9g 65%
Cholesterol 0mg 0%
Sodium 27mg 1%
Total Carbohydrate 15.4g 6%
Dietary Fiber 5.8g 21%
Total Sugars 7g
Protein 11.2g

Drink/Smoothie

Mango And Pineapple Smoothie

It is a very easy and great tasting smoothie, which is rich in nutrients and multivitamins.

Cook Time: 0 Minutes
Yield: 2 Servings

Ingredients

1 cup mango, chunks
1 cup pineapple, chunks
1 cup peach, pitted
2 frozen bananas, peeled
1-1/2 cup coconut milk

Directions

Dump all the ingredients in a blender and pulse for a few minutes.
Pour into ice-filled serving glasses and enjoy.

Nutrition Facts
Servings: 2
Amount per serving
Calories   501

% Daily Value*
Total Fat 29.6g 38%
Saturated Fat 25.6g 128%
Cholesterol 0mg 0%
Sodium 21mg 1%
Total Carbohydrate 63.8g 23%
Dietary Fiber 9.3g 33%
Total Sugars 44.8g
Protein 5.9g

Dessert

Pecan Ice Cream

It is a perfect plant-based, raw, and vegan recipe to devour. It is delicious ice cream for Paleo and a raw vegan diet.

Cook Time: 0 Minutes
Yield: 2 Servings

Ingredients
4 frozen bananas cut up & good frozen
1 tablespoon of agave syrup
½ teaspoon of vanilla
1 pinch of sea salt
1-1/3 cups of pecans

Directions

Place the frozen bananas inside a blender and pulse for 1 minute.
Place all the other ingredients, including pecans, agave nectar, and sea salt.
Pulse for a few seconds and add vanilla extract.
Once smooth in the paste, transfer to the bowl.
Freeze it for a few minutes, and serve.

Nutrition Facts
Servings: 3
Amount per serving
Calories 488
% Daily Value*
Total Fat 33.9g 43%
Saturated Fat 3.5g 18%
Cholesterol 0mg 0%
Sodium 84mg 4%
Total Carbohydrate 48.3g 18%
Dietary Fiber 9.1g 32%
Total Sugars 21g
Protein 6.7g

Day 16

Breakfast

Instant Pot Blueberry Coffee Cake

If you love coffee flavour then this cake fully satisfy your taste buds.

Cooking time: 20 minutes
Yield: 4 servings

Ingredients

2.5 cups almond flour
2 teaspoons baking soda
Pinch of salt
1/3 cup butter, softened
1/4 cup Stevia
3 eggs
½ cup coconut milk
10 ounces of fresh blueberries

Directions

Take a bunt pan and spray it with oil.

Take a small bowl and combine all dry ingredients.
Take a separate bowl and mix together egg with all the wet ingredients including berries.
Now mix well the ingredients of both the bowl.
Once batter is formed pour the batter into Bundt pan.
Pour 1-2 cups of water in the instant pot.
Set the trivet inside the pot.
Adjust Bundt pan on top of the trivet.
Lock the lid and set timer to 20 minutes.
Set a timer to 20 minutes at high.
Once the timer beeps release the steam naturally.
Afterward take out the Bundt pan.
Let the cake cool off by placing it on rack.
Then cut and serve.

Nutrition Facts
Servings: 4
Amount per serving
Calories   397
% Daily Value*
Total Fat 34.3g   44%
Saturated Fat 17.7g   89%
Cholesterol 163mg   54%
Sodium 834mg   36%
Total Carbohydrate 15.9g   6%
Dietary Fiber 4.3g   15%
Total Sugars 8.3g
Protein 9.3g

Lunch

Creamy Carrot Soup

It is a bold soupy recipe to enjoy as a lunch.

Cooking Time: 20-25 Minutes
Yield: 4 Servings

Ingredients

½ cup of cashews
2 onions, chopped
½ red bell pepper
1 pound carrots
1 teaspoon of rosemary
1 teaspoon of thyme
2 cloves garlic, minced
2 tablespoons lemon juice
Sea salt and black pepper, to taste

Directions

Take pre-soaked cashews and place them in a blender.
Make it in a smooth paste by adding the soaked water.

In a saucepan, add onions, carrots, rosemary, thyme, sage, bell pepper, and garlic.

Add water to the saucepan, and let it cook over medium heat for 15 minutes.

Remove the pan, and let the mixture get cool.

Pour the pan mixture to the blender and blend until a smooth paste is formed.

Add more water and then return to the saucepan.

Add lemon juice and adjust seasoning.

Boil until simmering

Serve hot.

Nutrition Facts

Servings: 4

Amount per serving

Calories 177

% Daily Value*

Total Fat 8.2g 10%

Saturated Fat 1.7g 8%

Cholesterol 0mg 0%

Sodium 85mg 4%

Total Carbohydrate 24g 9%

Dietary Fiber 5g 18%

Total Sugars 9.7g

Protein 4.5g

Dinner

Green And Potatoes With Corn Dressing

It is a very delicious and creamy dressing that gets its richness from the corn. It is a taste dressing served over green and potatoes.

Cooking Time: 0 Minutes
Yield: 4 Servings

Ingredients

12 ounces of golden yellow corn, frozen
4 tablespoons lemon juice
2 tablespoons fresh dill, finely chopped
½ teaspoon fresh chives, finely chopped
2 teaspoons Dijon-style mustard
½ teaspoon garlic powder
Salt and black pepper, to taste
4 potatoes, baked
2 cups of roasted green

Directions

Pour water in a blender and add corn.

Pulse it to make a smooth paste.
Then add the remaining ingredients.
Adjust seasoning and then chill it covered.
Once done, serve it over the roasted green and baked potatoes.

Nutrition Facts
Servings: 4
Amount per serving
Calories   577
% Daily Value*
Total Fat 11g   14%
Saturated Fat 4.2g   21%
Cholesterol 13mg   4%
Sodium 388mg   17%
Total Carbohydrate 111.6g   41%
Dietary Fiber 9g   32%
Total Sugars 6.4g
Protein 12.6g

Snack

Chickpea Avocado Salad

It is a flavorful salad that is not only delicious but also fills and nutritious.

Cooking Time: 0 Minutes
Yield: 4 Servings

Ingredients

2 cups cooked chickpeas, drained and rinsed
2 small red onion, peeled and diced small
3 cloves garlic, peeled
1 lime, juice and zest
2 jalapeño peppers, minced chopped cilantro
Sea salt to taste
2 avocados, coarsely chopped

Directions

Mix well all the ingredients in a large bowl and then serve.

Nutrition Facts
Servings: 4
Amount per serving
Calories 589
% Daily Value*
Total Fat 25.8g 33%
Saturated Fat 4.8g 24%
Cholesterol 0mg 0%
Sodium 274mg 12%
Total Carbohydrate 73.8g 27%
Dietary Fiber 25.2g 90%
Total Sugars 12.9g
Protein 21.8g

Drink/Smoothie

Green Banana Smoothie

It is a very organic and green drink that is full of antioxidants and vitamins.

Cooking Time: 0 Minutes
Yield: 3 Servings

Ingredients

2 large bananas, peeled, frozen
½ cup Greek yogurt
2 cups almond milk, unsweetened
1 cup baby spinach
¼ teaspoon vanilla extract
4 tablespoons almond butter
1 teaspoon of protein powder, plant-based

Directions

Smooth all the ingredients in a blender and pulse for 5 minutes.
Once done, pour it into ice-filled serving glasses and enjoy.

Nutrition Facts

Servings: 3

Amount per serving

Calories 774

% Daily Value*

Total Fat 55.1g 71%

Saturated Fat 38.2g 191%

Cholesterol 32mg 11%

Sodium 118mg 5%

Total Carbohydrate 43.3g 16%

Dietary Fiber 8.2g 29%

Total Sugars 25.8g

Protein 37g

Dessert

Pumpkin Tart With Oat Crust

It is a worthy dessert to enjoy on weekends; the addition of maple syrup gives it a sweet autumn flavor.

Cooking Time: 55 Minutes
Yield: 4 Serving

Ingredients

1-1/2 cups rolled oats
1 cup flaxseed meal, divided
6 tablespoons unsalted almond butter
1 cup unsweetened almond milk
16 ounces can pumpkin
1/3 cup chopped pitted whole dates
1/3 cup pure maple syrup
3 tablespoons arrowroot powder
4 teaspoons pumpkin pie spice
2 teaspoons pure vanilla extract
Pinch of salt

Directions

Preheat the oven to 400 degrees F.
Pulse oats, 2 tablespoons of flaxseed meal, and almond butter in a blender.
Cover and pulse until smooth.
Slow the running of a food processor and add milk.
Take out the mixture, and press it in a baking sheet to make a crust.
Now for the filling combine reaming flax meal with ¼ cup of water and let it sit for 5 minutes.
Add it to a food processor along with pumpkin, ¾ cup of milk, maple syrup, dates, arrowroot powder, pumpkin, pie spice, vanilla, and salt.
Process it until smooth.
Spread this filling into crust.
Bake in the oven for 50 to 55 minutes.
Serve.

Nutrition Facts
Servings: 2
Amount per serving
Calories   1415
% Daily Value*
Total Fat 74.3g   95%
Saturated Fat 6.6g   33%
Cholesterol 0mg   0%
Sodium 205mg   9%

Total Carbohydrate 153.4g 56%
Dietary Fiber 38.3g 137%
Total Sugars 65.5g
Protein 43.7g

Day 17

Breakfast

Banana French toast

It is a very spicy and aromatic twist to same old boring French toast.

Cooking Time: 15 Minutes
Yield: 3 Servings

Ingredients

1 banana
1 egg
1 pinch ground cloves
Pinch of nutmeg
3 pinches ground cinnamon
2 drops vanilla extra
1 pinch ground ginger
1 pinch ground cinnamon
6 slices bread

Directions

Take a shallow bowl and mash the bananas.

Whisk both eggs into the bowl along with the spices and vanilla extract.

Heat a frying pan.

Heat the oil in a frying pan.

Dip slices of bread in mixture and then transfer to pan for cooking.

Cook from both sides.

Once done, serve.

Enjoy.

Nutrition Facts

Servings: 2

Amount per serving

Calories 170

% Daily Value*

Total Fat 3.4g 4%

Saturated Fat 1g 5%

Cholesterol 82mg 27%

Sodium 216mg 9%

Total Carbohydrate 28.4g 10%

Dietary Fiber 2.5g 9%

Total Sugars 9.1g

Protein 5.5g

Lunch

Zoodles with Tofu And Peanut Sauce

The texture, taste, and aroma are scrumptious and beyond imagination.

Cooking Time: 15minutes
Yield: 4 Servings

Ingredients

4 zucchinis
350 grams firm tofu
1 tablespoon of sesame seeds, optional
2 tablespoons of olive oil

Ingredients For Peanut Sauce

1/3 cup peanut butter
1/3 cup water
1/3 cup soy sauce
4 tablespoons honey
2 tablespoons sesame oil clove garlic
2 tablespoons sriracha
Juice of 1 Lime

Directions

First, spiralize the zucchini.

Sprinkle the zucchini with salt and leave it for 30 minutes.

Rinse and drain then pat dry with a paper towel.

Make the peanut sauce by mixing all sauce ingredients into a food processor and blend it until creamy.

Drain and pat dry the tofu, then cut in cubes.

Heat olive oil in a pan, and add tofu.

Add in about half of the sauce and stir.

Once brown, remove the tofu from the pan and set aside.

Turn the pan heat to medium, and add zucchini noodles, and remaining sauce.

Once coated well, turn off the heat.

Combine all the ingredients in a bowl and serve.

Nutrition Facts

Servings: 4

Amount per serving

Calories   531

% Daily Value*

Total Fat 47.9g   61%

Saturated Fat 7.8g   39%

Cholesterol 0mg   0%

Sodium 1379mg   60%

Total Carbohydrate 15.9g   6%

Dietary Fiber 4.7g   17%
Total Sugars 6.3g
Protein 16.7g

Dinner

Roasted Potatoes

Cooking Time: 40 Minutes
Yield: 2 Servings

Ingredients

6 small russet or red potatoes
Salt and black pepper to taste

Directions

Heat the oven to 475 degrees F.
line a baking sheet with parchment paper.
Place the whole potatoes in a large pot, cover with water, and boil for 20 minutes or until just tender enough to pierce with a fork or knife.
Drain the potatoes and spread them evenly on the baking sheet.
Sprinkle the potatoes with salt and pepper.
place the baking sheet into the oven on the middle rack and roast for 30-40 minutes or until the potatoes are brown.
Serve.
 Nutrition Facts
Servings: 2

Amount per serving
Calories 357
% Daily Value*
Total Fat 0.7g 1%
Saturated Fat 0.2g 1%
Cholesterol 0mg 0%
Sodium 31mg 1%
Total Carbohydrate 81.1g 29%
Dietary Fiber 8.7g 31%
Total Sugars 5.1g
Protein 9.7g

Snack

Eggplant Dip

A perfect dip that is made with eggplants that gives it more flavor.

Cooking Time: 35 Minutes
Yield: 2 Servings

Ingredients

1-2 globe eggplants
3 tablespoons extra virgin olive oil
2 tablespoons tahini
1 tablespoon of lemon juice
Salt and cayenne pepper, to taste
2 garlic cloves, chopped
12 teaspoon cumin, ground

Directions

Heat the oven to 420°F.
Press the eggplants in different places from the fork.
 Cut the eggplants in two halves and then put olive oil on it.

Place the eggplants on the baking sheet, and bake it for about 35-40 minutes.

Take out from the oven and cool it for 12-15 minutes.

Scoop the eggplant flesh into a glass bowl and mash well with a fork

Add garlic, olive oil, cumin, tahini, lemon juice, salt, and cayenne.

Serve and enjoy.

Nutrition Facts

Servings: 2

Amount per serving

Calories 387

% Daily Value*

Total Fat 32.4g 42%

Saturated Fat 4.4g 22%

Cholesterol 0mg 0%

Sodium 45mg 2%

Total Carbohydrate 25g 9%

Dietary Fiber 12.4g 44%

Total Sugars 8.7g

Protein 7.5g

Drink/Smoothie

Raspberry Almond Chia Smoothie

It is a very healthy and mouthwatering glass of smoothie that is purely satisfying.

**Cooking Time: 0 Minutes
Yield: 2 Servings**

Ingredients

1 cup plain Greek yogurt
½ cup almond milk
¼ cup raspberries, frozen
¼ cup almonds, divided
2 tablespoons honey
1 Tablespoon Of Chia Seeds

Directions

Dump all the ingredients in a blender and pulse for 2 minutes.
Pour into serving glasses and enjoy.

Nutrition Facts
Servings: 2

Amount per serving
Calories 794
% Daily Value*
Total Fat 31.6g   41%
Saturated Fat 19.1g   96%
Cholesterol 60mg   20%
Sodium 310mg   13%
Total Carbohydrate 55.5g   20%
Dietary Fiber 6.9g   24%
Total Sugars 41.4g
Protein 74.6g

Dessert

Carrot and White Bean Vegan Blondie's

It is a very simple and yummy Blondie recipe that truly sits under the category of vegan, and a plant-based diet. It is a gluten-free recipe to enjoy.

Cooking Time: 25 Minutes
Yield: 4 Servings

Ingredients

1/3 cup old fashioned oats, ground
1/6 teaspoon salt
1/4 teaspoon baking powder
18 ounces of Great Northern beans, rinsed and drained
1/4 cup maple syrup
½ teaspoon vanilla extract
1/3 cup creamy peanut butter
½ cup shredded carrots
½ cup of chocolate chips

Directions

Preheat oven to 350 degrees F.
Grease a baking dish and set it aside.

Using a high-speed blender or food processor, grind the oats into flour.

Add the salt, vanilla extract, maple syrup, baking powder, peanut butter, beans, and shredded carrots to the oat flour.

Blend the ingredients at high speed for 3 minutes.

Pause the blender occasionally to stir the ingredients with a rubber spatula.

Pour the batter into the baking dish; spread it evenly with a rubber spatula.

Top with the chocolate chips.

Bake for 25 minutes.

Remove the pan from the oven.

The bars should be warm when they are cut into squares.

Serve.

Nutrition Facts

Servings: 4

Amount per serving

Calories   782

% Daily Value*

Total Fat 19.4g   25%

Saturated Fat 7.3g   36%

Cholesterol 5mg   2%

Sodium 242mg   11%

Total Carbohydrate 120g   44%

Dietary Fiber 29.4g 105%
Total Sugars 28.5g
Protein 36.7g

Day 18

Breakfast

Banana Bread

A very chewy, and flavorful bread that is super tasty and fit in the premises of plant based diet.

Cooking Time: 45 Minutes
Yield: 6 Servings

Ingredients

4 large bananas, ripe
½ teaspoon baking soda/baking power
1/4 cup ground flaxseed
1 1/3 cups whole wheat flour
1/3 cup maple syrup
1/3 cup apple sauce, unsweetened
1 teaspoon organic vanilla extract
Pinch of sea salt

Directions

Heat the oven to 370 degrees.

Place bananas into a bowl and mash it with the help of fork.

Next, pour the maple syrup, apple sauce, and vanilla extract to the bananas and mix well.

Add the flour, ground flaxseed, baking soda, and salt.

Stir well until all ingredients are thoroughly combined and make the batter.

Pour ingredients into nonstick standard-sized loaf pan.

You can also line a loaf pan with parchment paper if you like.

Bake bread for 45-50 minutes.

Slice, serve, and enjoy.

Nutrition Facts
Servings: 6
Amount per serving
Calories 805
% Daily Value*
Total Fat 48.3g 62%
Saturated Fat 29.8g 149%
Cholesterol 6mg 2%
Sodium 82mg 4%
Total Carbohydrate 86g 31%
Dietary Fiber 10.8g 38%
Total Sugars 26.4g
Protein 11.2g

Lunch

Zucchini, Corn, Soup

It is a luscious soup recipe that gives your taste buds a roller coaster ride of flavor with just a sip.

Cooking Time: 30 Minutes
Yield: 6 Servings

Ingredients

36 ounces of almond milk
2 cups russet potatoes, peeled and cubed
1/3 cup chopped onion
¼ cup chopped celery
4 cloves garlic, minced
1 cups fresh corn
16 ounces black beans, rinsed and drained
2 medium zucchinis, quartered lengthwise and cut into ¼-inch slices
½ teaspoon thyme
1 tablespoon sherry vinegar
Sea salt and black pepper, to taste

Directions

Take a medium Dutch oven and pour almond milk in it.
Then add onion, celery, potatoes, and garlic.
Bring the mixture to a boil for about 15 minutes.
Once potatoes are tender add corn, zucchini, thyme, and bean.
Return it to boil and simmer for 15 minutes.
Once all the ingredients are tender, add vinegar and season it with salt and pepper.
Serve and enjoy.

Nutrition Facts
Servings: 6
Amount per serving
Calories 723
% Daily Value*
Total Fat 42.1g 54%
Saturated Fat 36.3g 182%
Cholesterol 0mg 0%
Sodium 47mg 2%
Total Carbohydrate 73.2g 27%
Dietary Fiber 18.1g 65%
Total Sugars 10.2g
Protein 22.9g

Dinner

Vibrant Turmeric Coconut Rice

The vibrant color of rice is because of the addition of turmeric. This is a very aromatic recipe to enjoy.

Cooking Time: 35-40 Minutes
Yield: 4 Servings

Ingredients

2 cups long-grain white rice, such as jasmine
3 cups of coconut water
½ teaspoons turmeric, fresh
1/6 teaspoon fine sea salt
2 tablespoons coconut oil

Directions

Wash the rice under tap water and drain well.
After several times, the water will be clearer.
Return the rice to the saucepan.
Mix the rice, coconut water, turmeric, and salt in a nonstick saucepan.
Bring the mixture to a boil over high heat; stir it occasionally.

Decrease the heat, so the mixture is at a low boil for a few minutes; stir it occasionally.
Lower, cover the saucepan, and cook 10 minutes.
Turn off the heat; let the rice sit for 10 minutes.
Uncover the pan and add the coconut oil.
Fluff the rice to combine the ingredients.
Cover the pot again for 10 minutes.
Before serving, fluff the rice.
Pour the rice into serving plates.
Enjoy.

Nutrition Facts
Servings: 3
Amount per serving
Calories   575
% Daily Value*
Total Fat 10.4g   13%
Saturated Fat 8.5g   43%
Cholesterol 0mg   0%
Sodium 364mg   16%
Total Carbohydrate 107.7g   39%
Dietary Fiber 4.3g   15%
Total Sugars 6.4g
Protein 10.6g

Snack

Cauliflower Chocolate Pudding

A very nutritious and healthy recipe that is made with cauliflower and it is a true tasting recipe to enjoy.

Cooking Time: 0 Minutes
Yield: 4 Servings

Ingredients

4 cups cauliflower florets
3 cups non-dairy milk
½ cup of cacao powder
16 pitted Medjool dates
1 teaspoon vanilla extract

Directions

Steam the cauliflower enough till very tender.
Place all of the ingredients in a high-speed blender.
Blend the ingredients until they are smooth and creamy.
Serve.
 Nutrition Facts
Servings: 4
Amount per serving

Calories 738
% Daily Value*
Total Fat 8.7g 11%
Saturated Fat 4.1g 21%
Cholesterol 0mg 0%
Sodium 164mg 7%
Total Carbohydrate 171.9g 63%
Dietary Fiber 24.2g 87%
Total Sugars 124.5g
Protein 17.2g

Drink/Smoothie

Kiwi and Kale Smoothie

A super food like kale is part of this recipe that make it more flavorful and energetic.

Cooking Time: 5 Minutes
Yield: 4 Servings

Ingredients

1 cup of water, filtered
3 mangoes, peeled and pitted
4 kiwi fruits, peeled
2 cups kale, torn into pieces

Directions

Combine all the ingredients in a blender and pulse until smooth.
Serve into ice-filled glasses and enjoy.

Nutrition Facts
Servings: 4
Amount per serving
Calories   214

% Daily Value*
Total Fat 1.4g 2%
Saturated Fat 0.3g 1%
Cholesterol 0mg 0%
Sodium 21mg 1%
Total Carbohydrate 52.4g 19%
Dietary Fiber 6.8g 24%
Total Sugars 41.3g
Protein 3.9g

Dessert

Cornmeal Waffles

A perfect dessert time treat to enjoy with the addition of cornmeal, oats and whole wheat flour.

Cooking Time: 15 Minutes
Yield: 5 Servings

Ingredients

1 cup cornmeal
½ cup oats
2/3 cup whole wheat flour
½ teaspoon baking powder
½ teaspoon of sea salt
1 teaspoon ground cinnamon
½ cup almond or soy milk or other nut milk
1/3 cup applesauce
1 tablespoon maple syrup
1 tablespoon coconut oil optional
½ teaspoon vanilla extract non-alcoholic preferred

Blueberry Syrup

1 cup blueberries

2 tablespoons of maple syrup
2/3 cup chopped walnuts

Directions

Mix the wet ingredients, oil, milk, applesauce, maple syrup, and vanilla extract in a bowl.

In a separate bowl mix the dry ingredients, cornmeal, oats, flour, baking powder, salt, and cinnamon.

Pour the dry ingredients into the wet and combine carefully.

Cook in your waffle maker according to the directions.

To make blueberry syrup, pour a little maple syrup over the cup of blueberries and warm a few seconds in the microwave.

Top each waffle with a dollop of the blueberry/maple syrup mix, and a few walnuts.

Nutrition Facts
Servings: 5
Amount per serving
Calories   431
% Daily Value*
Total Fat 19.1g   25%
Saturated Fat 3.9g   19%
Cholesterol 0mg   0%
Sodium 200mg   9%

Total Carbohydrate 58.1g   21%
Dietary Fiber 6.5g   23%
Total Sugars 15g
Protein 11.1g

Day 19

Breakfast

Baked Oatmeal Cups

It is a perfect early Morning meal to enjoy, that uses unsweetened ingredients for natural taste and to make it a low calories breakfast

Cooking Time: 25 Minutes
Yield: 4 Servings

Ingredients

1 cup of applesauce, unsweetened
1 cup of butter
1 cup of almond milk
2-1/4 cups of organic rolled oats
1/3 hemp seeds
4 tablespoons of chia seeds
½ teaspoon of cinnamon
Salt, to taste

Directions

The oven should be preheated to 350ºF.
Use coconut oil to grease a large muffin pan.

With a whisk, combine the applesauce, butter, and milk.

When they are thoroughly mixed; stir in the oats, hemp seeds, chia seeds, cinnamon, and salt; Then mix it well.

Divide the batter evenly between the muffin cups.

Press the toppings lightly into the batter.

Bake it for 20-25 minutes.

Remove muffins from the pan after 10-15 minutes.

Use an airtight container to store any leftovers.

Enjoy.

Nutrition Facts

Servings: 4

Amount per serving

Calories 741

% Daily Value*

Total Fat 63.9g 82%

Saturated Fat 42.4g 212%

Cholesterol 122mg 41%

Sodium 379mg 16%

Total Carbohydrate 39g 14%

Dietary Fiber 6.7g 24%

Total Sugars 8.7g

Protein 8.2g

Lunch

Orange Black Bean Taquitos

It is a very delightful recipe that is zesty from the addition of orange zest .this recipe elevates the black beans to a new level.

Cooking Time: 20 Minutes
Yield: 10 Servings

Ingredients

2 small white onions, diced small
2 cloves garlic, minced
1 teaspoon cumin seeds, toasted and ground
2 chilies in adobo sauce, minced
2 oranges, zest, and juice
18 ounces black beans, drained and rinsed
Salt, to taste
20 corn tortillas
2 cups Sour Cream
1 cup of salsa

Directions

Take a saucepan and sauté onions in it for 10 minutes.
Add water about a teaspoon to keep onions away from sticking.
Next add garlic, cumin and chili adobo sauce.
Then add orange zest and juice along with black beans.
Season it with salt.
Now puree this mixture in the food processor.
Heat the tortilla in the skillet.
Now stack tortilla with the blended mixture.
Top it with the addition of sour cream and salsa.
Enjoy.
Nutrition Facts
Servings: 10
Amount per serving
Calories   414
% Daily Value*
Total Fat 12.1g   15%
Saturated Fat 6.4g   32%
Cholesterol 20mg   7%
Sodium 269mg   12%
Total Carbohydrate 63.4g   23%
Dietary Fiber 12.8g   46%
Total Sugars 6.8g
Protein 16.2g

Dinner

Rise Sweet Potato Dinner Rolls

The sweetness of the dinner rolls in because of sweetness from the mashed potatoes. These dinner rolls are made from whole grains and very moist and delicious.

Cooking Time: 25 Minutes
Yield: 4 Servings

Ingredients

4 cups of whole wheat flour, divided
2 packages quick-rising yeast
¼ teaspoon of sea salt
1-1/2 cups mashed sweet potato
1 cup unsweetened applesauce
1/3 cup unsweetened almond milk
4 tablespoons pure cane sugar

Directions

Take a bowl and add flour, salt, and yeast.
In a bowl, stir potatoes, milk, applesauce, and sugar.
Warm the mixture at 120 degrees F for 5 minutes.

Then add the sweet potato mixture to the flour mixture.
Beat the mixer for 30 seconds.
Stir in more flour, if needed and mix well.
Make the dough and knead it on a flat surface.
Cover and let it rest for 10 minutes.
Line a baking sheet with parchment paper.
Divide the dough into equal portions.
Roll the portions in the ball and place them on a baking sheet.
Let it rise for a few more minutes.
Bake it in the oven for 25 minutes, at 400 depress F.
Serve and enjoy warm.

Nutrition Facts
Servings: 4
Amount per serving
Calories   589
% Daily Value*
Total Fat 1.8g 2%
Saturated Fat 0.3g   1%
Cholesterol 0mg   0%
Sodium 185mg   8%
Total Carbohydrate 126.6g   46%
Dietary Fiber 6g   21%
Total Sugars 18g
Protein 15.7g

Snack

Eggplant Caviar

The true flavors of the Middle East are introducing this recipe.

Cooking Time: 4 Hours
Yield: 4 Servings

Ingredients

2 pounds of eggplant
1 cup tomato, chopped
½ cup onion, chopped
1 cup of full-fat Greek yogurt
4 cloves of garlic, minced
4 tablespoons olive oil
1 teaspoon dried oregano leaves
1 tablespoon lemon juice
Salt and black pepper, to taste

Directions

Pierce the eggplant with a fork add then place it in the slow cooker.
Cover the slow cooker and cook for 4 hours.

Then take out the eggplant and let it get cool.
Cut the eggplant and scoop out eh pulp.
Mash pulp in a bowl and add remaining ingredients.
Mix well and serve.

Nutrition Facts
Servings: 2
Amount per serving
Calories 874
% Daily Value*
Total Fat 38.2g 49%
Saturated Fat 10.1g 51%
Cholesterol 60mg 20%
Sodium 317mg 14%
Total Carbohydrate 62.5g 23%
Dietary Fiber 18.2g 65%
Total Sugars 38.5g
Protein 75.1g

Drink/Smoothie

Melon-Mango Smoothie

The combination of cantaloupe and mangos goes well in this smoothie recipe that provides extra nutrition and health.

Cooking Time: 5 Minutes
Yield:2 Servings

Ingredients

1 cup of water, filtered
2 cups cantaloupe, cubed
2 cups mangos, peeled and pitted
2 cups baby spinach, washed

Directions

Blend all the ingredients in the blender for a smooth paste.
Serve into ice-filled glasses and enjoy.

Nutrition Facts
Servings: 2
Amount per serving

Calories 159
% Daily Value*
Total Fat 1.1g 1%
Saturated Fat 0.3g 1%
Cholesterol 0mg 0%
Sodium 54mg 2%
Total Carbohydrate 38.5g 14%
Dietary Fiber 4.7g 17%
Total Sugars 34.9g
Protein 3.5g

Dessert

Raw Chocolate Coconut Cashew Bars

It is a very easy, organic, and healthy recipe to enjoy as dessert. It is a pure plant-based and dairy-free dessert recipe.

Cooking Time: 0 Minutes
Yield:6 Servings

Ingredients

2 cups cashews
1-1/2 cups oats, old fashioned
½ cup of coconut oil
½ cup honey
Salt, to taste

Ingredients For Topping

½ cup of honey
½ cup of coconut oil
1 cup cocoa powder, unsweetened
4 tablespoons of roasted coconut flakes, unsweetened
¼ teaspoon or a pinch of salt

Directions

Line a loaf pan on a baking pan with parchment paper.
Coat the parchment paper with cooking spray.
Set it aside.
Put the cashews in a food processor and pulse.
Add in the oats, coconut oil, honey, and sea salt; process for 2 minutes.
Press the dough into the pan; spread evenly to the edges of the pan.
Prepare the chocolate topping by whisking together all of the ingredients in a glass bowl.
Pour the chocolate mixture over the dough; spread it evenly.
Freeze the dough for 1 hour.
Then slice and serve.
Enjoy.

Nutrition Facts
Servings: 6
Amount per serving
Calories   842
% Daily Value*
Total Fat 61.4g   79%
Saturated Fat 37.9g   189%
Cholesterol 0mg   0%
Sodium 41mg 2%

Total Carbohydrate 79.1g 29%
Dietary Fiber 7.4g 27%
Total Sugars 49.3g
Protein 11.7g

Day 20

Breakfast

Vegan Breakfast Skillet

It is one of the highly satisfying recipes that include almost all healthy vegetables. This recipe is rich in vitamins, protein, minerals, and nutrients.

Cooking Time: 25-30 Minutes
Yield: 6 Servings

Ingredients

½ cup of coconut oil
6 potatoes, pieces
1/3 red pepper
1/3 green pepper
1/3 yellow pepper
1/3 orange pepper
1 onion, chopped
1 cup mushrooms (optional)
½ cup spinach, chopped
Salt and black pepper, to taste
3 teaspoons Italian seasoning
2 teaspoons garlic powder
4 tablespoons of maple syrup

Directions

Cut the potatoes into equal size pieces.
Soak them in water for 30 minutes.
While the potatoes are soaking, cut up the peppers and onions into equal size pieces.
Dice the mushrooms, if desired.
Drain the potatoes and pat them dry with a towel.
Melt the coconut oil in a large skillet over medium-high heat.
Place the potatoes into the skillet in a single layer.
Cook for 5 minutes; flip and cook for another 5 minutes.
Stir the ingredients again; cook for an additional 5 minutes.
Reduce heat to medium-low.
Stir in the peppers and onions.
Add in all the seasonings: stir to combine.
Stir in the the maple syrup over everything; cook until spinach has wilted.
Serve and enjoy.

Nutrition Facts
Servings: 6
Amount per serving
Calories   365
% Daily Value*
Total Fat 19.2g   25%

Saturated Fat 15.9g   79%
Cholesterol 2mg   1%
Sodium 23mg 1%
Total Carbohydrate 47g   17%
Dietary Fiber 6.1g   22%
Total Sugars 12.3g
Protein 4.6g

Lunch

Quinoa Gado-Gado Bowl

A perfect and modern twist a Gado Gado bowl, as we replace the quinoa for rice and add some healthy vegetables as to make it a plant-based treat to enjoy

Cooking Time: 25 Minutes
Yield: 2 Servings

Ingredients

GADO-GADO ingredients

2 cups of green beans, trimmed
1 cup red quinoa, rinsed
½ cup mung bean sprouts
21/2 cups red cabbage
3 carrots

SAUCE Ingredients

½ cup peanut butter, creamy
2 tablespoons of tamari sauce
4 tablespoons of maple syrup, or to taste
4 tablespoons of lemon or lime juice
1 teaspoon of chili garlic sauce

6 tablespoons of water

Directions

Toast the quinoa in a small pan using medium heat for 3-4 minutes, stir it frequently.

Stir in water, and let it start to boil.

Then lower the heat to a simmer; cover the pan and cook the quinoa for 18-20 minutes (the liquid should be absorbed; the quinoa tender).

Turn off the heat, remove the lid, and fluff the quinoa with a fork.

Meanwhile, steam green beans, carrots, and cabbage in the microwave or steamer basket (over 1" of water using medium-high heat), approximately 4 minutes in the steamer.

When the beans complete steaming, put them in ice water to stop cooking; set aside.

Make peanut sauce by whisking together all of the ingredients, except the water; add the water in increments of 1 tablespoon to create a semi-thick sauce.

Adjust the flavor as needed, adding more tamari, lime juice, maple syrup, and/or chili garlic sauce.

Divide the quinoa between 2 serving bowls.

serve

Offer the peanut sauce on the side and any additional toppings you desire.

Nutrition Facts
Servings: 2
Amount per serving
Calories 347
% Daily Value*
Total Fat 1.6g 2%
Saturated Fat 0.2g 1%
Cholesterol 0mg 0%
Sodium 148mg 6%
Total Carbohydrate 79.6g 29%
Dietary Fiber 16.4g 59%
Total Sugars 42.4g
Protein 11.6g

Dinner

Vegetable Spaghetti

It is a very healthy dinner that keeps you full until the next morning.

Cooking Time: 25 Minutes
Yield: 4 Servings

Ingredients

12 ounces spaghetti, brown rice
2 green bell pepper, cubed small
4 plum tomatoes, sliced
Salt, to taste
1 jalapeño, chopped
4 tablespoons herbes de Provence, dried
2 tablespoons tomato purée
2 tablespoons lime juice
5 red or cherry tomatoes, chopped
1/2 zucchini, sliced
2.5 bunch of spinach, chopped
½ cup of green or black olives

Directions

Follow the package directions to cook the spaghetti.

when done, drain it in a colander.

Combine the plum tomatoes, peppers, salt, jalapeño and herbes de Provence in a saucepan.

Pour ¼ cup water and simmer; it will create the sauce.

After 2 minutes, stir in the tomato purée and lime juice.

When the peppers and tomatoes have simmered down, add the tomatoes, zucchini, and spinach.

Stir the ingredients thoroughly; cook approximately 10 minutes.

Add the olives, pasta and a bit more of the herbes de Provence into the sauce.

Place it into a serving dish and serve.

Nutrition Facts
Servings: 4
Amount per serving
Calories 868
% Daily Value*
Total Fat 45.9g 59%
Saturated Fat 5.9g 29%
Cholesterol 62mg 21%
Sodium 796mg 35%
Total Carbohydrate 72.1g 26%
Dietary Fiber 27.8g 99%
Total Sugars 12.7g
Protein 48.6g

Snack

Sushi Salad

If you love the flavor of sushi then this salad is just for you. It is much healthier than sushi and lowers in calories as well.

Cooking Time: 2 Minutes
Yield: 6 Servings

Ingredients

Rice Bowl Ingredients

3 cups edamame beans, frozen shelled
5 cups brown rice, cooked
5 cucumbers, sliced
4 avocados,
1 cup of baby spinach leaves
2 tablespoons of olive oil
2 tablespoons sesame seeds
6 Nori seaweed sheets, strips
Salt and black pepper, to taste

Ingredients For Sesame And Miso Dressing

4 tablespoons Miso paste

2 tablespoons toasted sesame oil
½ tablespoon Mirin
½ teaspoon sugar

Directions

Add salt to the water in a pot.
Bring it to a boil and stir in the beans.
Cook for approximately 1-2 minutes.
Drain the beans in a colander then cool using cold water.
For the dressing, whisk together all the ingredients, and a little water (1-2 tablespoons); mix until creamy.
Add the sesame seeds; stir to combine.
In a large bowl, mix the rice, beans, cucumber, avocado, and spinach; toss the salad gently.
Transfer the salad to a serving bowl.
Drizzle the sesame–Miso dressing onto the salad and season to taste with sea salt and black pepper.
Use the sesame seeds and Nori strips for topping.
Nutrition Facts
Servings: 4
Amount per serving
Calories 1569
% Daily Value*
Total Fat 64.9g 83%

Saturated Fat 12.2g 61%
Cholesterol 0mg 0%
Sodium 1021mg 44%
Total Carbohydrate 225.5g 82%
Dietary Fiber 26.7g 95%
Total Sugars 10.1g
Protein 30.9g

Drink/Smoothie

Grapefruit and Pineapple Smoothie

Cooking Time: 0 Minutes
Yield: 2 Servings

Ingredients

1 cup almond milk
2 fresh bananas, peeled and sliced
1 red grapefruit, peeled and seedless
1 cup pineapple, cubed
1/4 cup fresh parsley

Directions

Dump all the ingredients in a high-speed blender.
Pulse it for 6 minutes.
Once smooth, pour into glasses and enjoy.

Nutrition Facts
Servings: 2
Amount per serving
Calories   445
% Daily Value*
Total Fat 29.2g   37%

Saturated Fat 25.5g   128%
Cholesterol 0mg   0%
Sodium 24mg 1%
Total Carbohydrate 50.1g   18%
Dietary Fiber 7.8g   28%
Total Sugars 31.1g
Protein 5.1g

Dessert

Sweet & Salty Healthy Dessert Bars

It is a sweet and a bit salty tasting recipe to enjoy.

Cooking Time: 5 Minutes
Yields: 5 Servings

Ingredients

For The Base

1 cup almonds
½ cup unsweetened coconut flakes
1-1/3 cup of rolled oats
6 tablespoons of coconut oil
2 tablespoons maple syrup

For The Caramel

1 teaspoon of maple syrup
1-1/2 cup Medjool dates pitted
4 tablespoons of tahini
4 tablespoons of coconut oil
Sea salt

Ingredients For The Chocolate

150 grams of vegan dark chocolate
3 teaspoons coconut oil

Directions

Line a medium loaf pan with parchment paper or aluminum foil; coat it with cooking spray and set aside.

Bring a small saucepan of water to a boil then turn off the heat.

Put the dates in the water for 10-20 minutes.

Put the almonds, coconut, and oats in a food processor; pulse the ingredients until they become a coarse powder.

Add the coconut oil & maple syrup; process the mixture until it forms the dough.

Put the prepared dough into the loaf pan.

Put the pan inside the refrigerator or freezer.

Clean the food processor.

Add the ingredients for the caramel to the food processor.

Process the ingredients until they are smooth and creamy.

Pour over the layer in the loaf pan.

Return to the freezer.

Melt the chocolate along with the coconut oil in the microwave.
Pour the chocolate evenly over the caramel layer.
You may sprinkle some sea salt on top if desired
Return to the freezer for at least 15 minutes.
Cut the loaf into 8-9 slices with a very sharp knife; cut each of those pieces in half.
Then, cut each of those in half.
Serve.

Nutrition Facts
Servings: 5
Amount per serving
Calories 948
% Daily Value*
Total Fat 70.9g 91%
Saturated Fat 46.6g 233%
Cholesterol 7mg 2%
Sodium 40mg 2%
Total Carbohydrate 75.2g 27%
Dietary Fiber 11.8g 42%
Total Sugars 45.2g
Protein 13.3g

Day 21

Breakfast

Banana Teff Bread

It is healthy, nourishing and nutritious healthy bread recipe to enjoy

Cooking Time: 40 Minutes
Yield: 6 Servings

Ingredients

3 ripe bananas, peeled
1/3 cup of almond milk
3 teaspoons apple cider vinegar
1 teaspoon pure vanilla extract
1 cup teff flour
4 tablespoons pure cane sugar
1/3 cup chopped walnuts
2 teaspoons baking powder
¼ teaspoon baking soda
1/4 teaspoon ground cinnamon
1 pinch of sea salt
20 raisins, soaked and drained

Directions

Preheat the oven to 375 degrees F.
Take a silicon pan and layer it with parchment paper.
In a bowl, mash bananas and add in the milk, vanilla, and vinegar.
In a separate bowl, add the next eight ingredients.
Add milk mixture to the dry flour mixture.
Fold the ingredients together well.
Bake it in the oven for 40 minutes.
Once done, serve.
Enjoy.
Nutrition Facts
Servings: 3
Amount per serving
Calories   930
% Daily Value*
Total Fat 17.1g   22%
Saturated Fat 6.3g   32%
Cholesterol 0mg   0%
Sodium 217mg   9%
Total Carbohydrate 198.3g   72%
Dietary Fiber 16.5g   59%
Total Sugars 118.3g
Protein 15.9g

Lunch

Harvest Vegetable Instant Pot Minestrone

It is a hearty and healthy pasta dish that is made with organic ingredients.

Cooking Time: 30 Minutes
Yield: 4 Servings

Ingredients

1 cup chopped onions
½ cup dried white beans (any variety), rinsed and drained
2 cloves garlic, minced
1 cup carrots
½ cup celery
½ cup parsnips
½ cup turnip
1 cup rutabaga
¼ teaspoon dried oregano, crushed
4 cups dried shell pasta
18 ounces of tomato paste
Sea salt and freshly ground black pepper, to taste

Directions

Take an instant pot, and add onions, bean, and garlic.
Add in 3 cups of water and lock the lid of the instant pot.
Set timer to 40 minutes.
Once the timer beeps, release the pressure naturally for 10 minutes.
 Now open the pot and add six ingredients through oregano.
Cook on sauté mode for10 minuets.
Now add pasta and water.
 Uncover and cook for 10 more minutes.
Adjust seasoning and serve.
Nutrition Facts
Servings: 5
Amount per serving
Calories   1966
% Daily Value*
Total Fat 15g   19%
Saturated Fat 2.2g   11%
Cholesterol 449mg   150%
Sodium 303mg   13%
Total Carbohydrate 378.3g   138%
Dietary Fiber 10.1g   36%
Total Sugars 17.8g
Protein 79.8g

Dinner

Low Carb Easy Soup

It is a very low calories soup to enjoy.teh addition of bok Choy make is yummy soup. We have replaced soy sauce with coconut amino for much better taste and flavor. It is a hearty and mouthwatering soup recipe to enjoy any time you liked.

**Cooking Time: 15 Minutes
Yield: 3 Servings**

Ingredients

½ pound Bok Choy
2 tablespoons vegetable oil
1 cup mushrooms
2 cups tofu, cooked and diced
4 tablespoons coconut amino
6 cups vegetable broth, unsalted
2 tablespoons fresh spinach, shredded
2 green onions, chopped (optional)
Salt and black pepper, to taste

Directions

Take a large pot and place it over medium flame.
Add oil to the pot and add bok Choy and mushrooms.
Let it cook for 4 minutes.
Next, pour vegetable broth and coconut amino.
Bring the mixture to boil.
Then add spinach and tofu.
 Cook for 2 more minutes.
Season the soup with salt and black pepper.
Top it with green onions and serve.
Nutrition Facts
Servings: 4
Amount per serving
Calories   220
% Daily Value*
Total Fat 14.3g   18%
Saturated Fat 3g   15%
Cholesterol 0mg   0%
Sodium 1200mg   52%
Total Carbohydrate 5.9g   2%
Dietary Fiber 2.1g   8%
Total Sugars 2.9g
Protein 19.2g

Snack

Chocolate Chip Cookies

Once you have a bit of these yummy cookies, you can't stop eating it.

**Cooking Time: 20 Hours
Servings: 5**

Ingredients

10 tablespoons butter, melted
2 eggs, whisked
1 teaspoon vanilla extract
1/3 cup stevia
1 cup almond meal/flour
1 teaspoon baking powder
1/4 teaspoon salt
½ cup unsweetened chocolate morsels
½ cup almonds
½ cup walnuts
Oil spray for greasing

Directions

Preheat oven at 350 degrees F.

Whisk egg in a bowl and add melted butter, salt, and vanilla extract to it

Fluff it and add stevia.

Next, add almonds and walnuts.

Next, mix almond flour and baking soda to the mixture.

In the end, add chocolate morsels.

Oil sprays a baking sheet and pour a spoon full of the mixture to the pan.

Place it inside the oven and bake for15-20 minutes.

Once cookies are ready, take out and serve.

Nutrition Facts

Servings: 4

Amount per serving

Calories   596

% Daily Value*

Total Fat 58.3g   75%

Saturated Fat 20.9g   104%

Cholesterol 158mg   53%

Sodium 237mg   10%

Total Carbohydrate 10.3g   4%

Dietary Fiber 5.6g   20%

Total Sugars 2.2g

Protein 14.4g

Drink/Smoothie

Strawberry-Orange Smoothie

It is a delicious smoothie that is full of antioxidants and potassium. One glass of smoothie is enough to satisfy your mid day cravings.

Cooking Time: 0 Minutes
Yield: 2 Servings

Ingredients

1 cup of almond milk
4 bananas, peeled and sliced
1 cup of strawberries
1oranges, de-seeded
Ice cubes, for chilling

Directions

Blend all the ingredients in a blender until a smooth consistency is obtained.
Serve into ice-filled glasses.
Enjoy chilled.
Nutrition Facts

Servings: 2
Amount per serving
Calories 552
% Daily Value*
Total Fat 29.7g 38%
Saturated Fat 25.6g 128%
Cholesterol 0mg 0%
Sodium 21mg 1%
Total Carbohydrate 76.9g 28%
Dietary Fiber 12.4g 44%
Total Sugars 45g
Protein 6.7g

Dessert

Peach-Cranberry Cobbler

It is a delicious cobbler recipe that has tart flavor because of the addition of cranberries. It is best served over ice-cream.

Cooking Time: 35 Minutes
Yield: 6 Servings

Ingredients

½ cup pure cane sugar
2 tablespoons cornstarch
18 ounces of peach slices, thawed
1-1/2 cup cranberries
1-1/2 cup whole rolled oats
1/3 cup honey
2 tablespoons chia seeds
2 teaspoons baking powder
1/3 teaspoon ground cinnamon
¼ cup unsweetened almond milk
1/3 cup unsweetened applesauce
1/3 cup cashew butter

Directions

Preheat the oven to 375 degrees F.
Heat a saucepan and add ½ cup of sugar, along with corn starch, and some water.
Add peaches and cook it over medium heat.
Then add cranberries and cook.
Next for topping mix oats, honey, chia seed, cinnamon, baking powder, almond milk, applesauce, and cashew butter.
Add this mixture to the top of the peaches.
Bake it in the oven for 20 minutes.
Once fluffy and bubbly, serve and enjoy.

Nutrition Facts
Servings: 6
Amount per serving
Calories   978
% Daily Value*
Total Fat 9.2g 12%
Saturated Fat 1.5g   8%
Cholesterol 0mg   0%
Sodium 13mg 1%
Total Carbohydrate 89g   32%
Dietary Fiber 9.3g   33%
Total Sugars 75.7g
Protein 7.9g

Shopping List for 21 Day Meal Plan

The proper meal plan takes planning but not requires a great deal of time. Once you have a clear idea or road map to follow, you can head to the market and focus on the mission that helps save your time and help you get the best food you needed for 21 days meal plan. It recommended bringing the grocery bag straight to the vegetable section. When you stop to see what going around like sales on items, actually, you are wasting your time and energy. You should have a work plan, and these advertisements shouldn't derail you.

- ➢ Create the grocery list to get value for money.
- ➢ Look for the recipes that matter for that particle week and then get the list of ingredients to be brought from the store.
- ➢ Buy enough food to prepare the meal.
- ➢ Make sure to fall within budget
- ➢ Be fast and efficient.

Shopping list

- ➢ Almond Milk
- ➢ Almond Flour
- ➢ Apple Sauce

- Maple Syrup, Pure
- Cinnamon Powder
- Salt
- Orange Zest
- Whole-Grain Bread Slices
- Raspberries
- Sweet Potato
- Chickpeas
- Cilantro
- Brown Rice
- Beets
- Brussels sprouts
- Carrot Juice
- Green Lentils
- Red Lentils
- Kidney Beans
- Tomato Sauce
- Peanut Butter
- Chick Peas
- Olive Oil
- Tamari Sauce
- Agave Nectar
- Apple
- Pineapple
- Hemp Seed
- Chocolate
- Maple Sugar
- Cocoa Powder, Unsweetened

- Buckwheat Flour
- Broccoli
- Bok Choy
- Five-Spice Powder
- Snow Peas
- Pinto Beans
- Dijon Mustard
- Ketchup
- Garlic
- Chilli Powder
- Pineapple Chunks
- Green Cabbage, Sliced
- Radishes, Sliced
- Tortillas
- Pistachios
- Vanilla Protein Powder
- Kale
- Berries, Frozen
- Dates, Pitted
- Oat Flour
- Walnuts
- Cocoa Powder
- Green Onion
- Firm Raw Tofu
- Red Tomato
- Turmeric
- Rye Bread, Toasted
- Sesame Seeds

- Green Zucchinis
- Garlic Powder
- Turnip
- Coconut Milk
- Swiss chard
- Brussels Sprout
- Green Gram Split, Pre-Soaked
- Tahini
- Blueberries, Frozen
- Almond Extract
- Whole Wheat Pastry Flour
- Cocoa Powder
- Raspberries
- Spelt Flour
- Eggs
- Cashew Milk
- Blueberries
- Whole Wheat Pasta, Penne
- Leeks
- Chives
- White Wine Vinegar
- Rolled Oats
- Protein Powder
- Clementines
- Almond Butter
- Spelt Flour
- Cocoa Powder
- Pumpkin Puree

- Cashew Milk
- Cinnamon
- Cacao Powder
- Natural Peanut Butter
- Whole-Grain Bread
- Quinoa
- Chilli Powder
- Black Beans
- Cherry Tomatoes
- Cabbage
- Avocados, Sliced
- Brussels sprouts
- Cauliflower
- Carrots
- Turnips
- Beets
- Sweet Potatoes
- Balsamic Vinegar
- Honey
- Rosemary
- Fresh Figs
- Walnuts, Chopped
- Blueberries, Frozen
- Sunflower Seed
- Quinoa, Pre-Soaked
- Cashew Cream, Unsweetened
- Chickpea Flour
- Nutritional Yeast

- Mushrooms
- Black Olives
- Cream
- Acorn Squashes
- Shallots
- Mushrooms
- Cranberries
- Asparagus
- Whole Wheat Bread Crumbs
- Protein Powder
- Almonds
- Maca Powder
- Organic Hemp Seeds
- Cherries
- Blueberries
- Chickpea Flour
- Italian Seasoning
- Rosemary
- Soba Noodles
- Red Bell Pepper
- Scallions
- Light Soy Sauce
- Raw Peanuts
- Cumin Powder
- Red Chilli Powder
- Coconut Oil
- Cocoa Powder
- Peanut Butter

- Raspberries
- Banana
- Roma Tomato
- Pumpkin
- Flaxseed Meal
- Pumpkin Pie Spice
- Cannellini Beans
- Black Olives
- Raisins
- Mangos
- Peach, Fresh
- Peanut Butter
- Avocados
- Pumpkin Seeds
- Tofu
- Cucumber
- Tamari Sauce
- Sesame Oil
- Blueberries, Frozen
- Granola
- Cabbage
- Kale
- Mustard Seeds
- Curry Powder
- Oranges
- Pomegranate
- Buttermilk
- Penne Pasta

- Green Beans
- Jalapeno
- white Wine Vinegar
- Basil
- Garbanzo Beans
- Parsley Leaves
- Sesame Seeds
- Chives
- Potatoes
- Gelatine Powder
- Heavy Whipping Cream
- Pomegranate
- Raspberry Jam
- Cane Sugar
- Whole Wheat Pastry Flour
- Cocoa Powder
- Chipotle Powder
- Corn Chips
- Soy Sauce
- Green Onion
- Pickled Onions
- Peach
- Cranberry
- Bok Choy
- Rutabaga
- Sesame Oil
- Red Cabbage
- Collard Greens

- Edamame Beans
- Seaweed Sheet
- Miso Paste
- Mirin
- Spaghetti
- Cantaloupe
- Arrowroot Powder
- Tortillas
- Sherry Vinegar
- Greek Yogurt
- Cornmeal
- Kiwi
- Sour Cream

Conclusion

Congratulations on embarking on a mouth-watering journey of a plant-based diet for 21 days.

All the myths are busted, and long gone are those days when people find it hard to lose weight. We have introduced this revolutionary diet plane of 21 days that helps you achieve your weight loss goal and give you more energy, better appearance, and stamina.

Unlike some other diet plans that seem like a marketing gambit, the plant-based diet plan not only helps lose weight but also provides the body with all the nutrients along with compromising taste and texture. If you are a meat lover, it's not hard to follow a plant-based diet, as it doesn't omit any meat items, but limit the proportion size.

The 21 days diet plan serves the whole day well by introducing breakfast to the dinner meals, and also includes snacks and desserts. Eating a bowl of vegetable become fun when following a plant-based diet. These comprehensive books provide you with a wide variety of meals that you can include in your daily routine to have a roller coaster ride of flavors. Recipes are healthy, low calories, and perfect to keep the obesity at bay. No excuse comes when following a plant-based diet, as it is not at all a complex process. The ingredients included in the book are easily available, and meals are prepared in the easiest way possible.

This book will surely help you gain the willpower to resist junk food items. It helps you to keep in mind overall calorie intake. It helps you to cut meat, bad fat, and carbohydrates from your plate. You just need to focus on what is plant-based, organic, whole, unprocessed, and healthy. To help you choose the best plant-based ingredients, we have introduced this book.

Whether you are a busy mother or professional, you can make a hearty plant-based diet and eat it on the go or right away.

Finally, if you found this book useful in any way, a review on Amazon is always appreciated!

Printed in Great Britain
by Amazon